My 30's and 40's Childhood

Ray Wooster

TSL Publications

First published in Great Britain in 2019
By TSL Publications, Rickmansworth

Copyright © 2019 Ray Wooster

ISBN / 978-1-912416-88-2

This is a collection of my childhood memories
during the 1930s and 1940s.
I grew up in Greenford and Northolt in the
county of Middlesex.
Some of my memories are humorous and
some are sad, but all are true.
I hope you will find them interesting.

My 1930's Boyhood

Why? Why? Why?

'Why did Tom fall down when the man went bang Mummy?'

'How did you know that Tom fell down? I sent you to your room.'

'I looked out of the window and I saw what happened.'

My poor Mother, outsmarted by a three year old!

It was just after breakfast. I was out in the yard throwing sticks and balls for Ben and Buster, the yard dogs, and also Floss, our house dog. Everywhere that Raymond went, Floss was sure to go!

When the knacker man drove into the yard, the driver wound down his window, 'Is your Mum or Dad about sonny?'

'My Dad's at work, but my Mum's indoors. I will fetch her as soon as I have put the dogs in the shed.'

'Good boy.'

I grabbed Ben and Buster's collars and they allowed me to steer them into the shed.

Whenever a car or lorry came into the yard, I begged a ride down to Oldfield Lane, my Mother would wait for me at the gate. Before I could beg my ride my Mother said, 'This gentleman is not allowed to have more than two people in the cab at any time, isn't that right driver?'

'Indeed it is Missis Wooster, just me and my mate. More than my job's worth to 'ave anyone else in the cab. Maybe some other time eh?'

'Now Raymond go to your room. The driver is going to manoeuvre his lorry and he doesn't want to run you over.'

The driver jumped down from his cab and pointed to the house. 'Just for me eh,' he said.

I was going to suggest that the driver's mate walked to the corner, but thought better of it.

Walking back to the house, I recalled the words I heard last night whilst siting on the back step. Joe Hutt and my Dad were in the kitchen talking about a horse, a very sick horse.

'You're doing the right thing Guv'nor. If 'e goes down you'll never get him up agin and if 'e blows, well, yer might as well take a box a matches to the place because no one will come near nor buy the place. Jobs are 'ard to find but not that 'ard.'

'Thank you for your opinion Joe. I value it so much so, that I am prepared to spare you a bottle of Gwen's elderberry wine. Here put it out of sight in your bag. If you fall off your bike, save the wine.'

Joe laughed, 'Trust me guv, trust me.'

I moved off the step as I didn't want Joe to trip over me.

'Good night Mr Hutt.'

'Night young Raymond, see you tomorrow.'

As I watched Joe cycle out of the yard I said, 'Mr Hutt is a nice man, isn't he Dad?'

There were no other children where we lived except for the little girl next door, who would stare wistfully out of her bedroom window. When I beckoned her to come and play, she would shake her head and get down from the window ledge. I would wait a while just in case her Mother let her out, not that I was at a loss for things to do.

Opposite our cottages the workmen were building a row of maisonettes and they needed all the help they could get.

A shout would go up, 'Ere 'e comes with 'is wooden 'orse 'n cart.'

Not only did I take sand to the man mixing cement, I also ran errands to the shop on the corner. It wasn't a shop, more of a wooden shack. The tea boy would take orders from the men and place the list in a patchwork bag which was almost as big as me and off I would go.

My Mother remonstrated with the foreman when I told her of my errands and the penny that I got for going.

'Don't you worry Missis – there's at least three pairs of eyes a watchin' 'im, all the way there an' all the way back,' the foreman reassured her.

My career in the building trade nearly came to an end when I insisted that I take my meals on site with the workmen. The tea boy showed me how to make bucket tea, much better than the stuff that comes out of a teapot.

This is what you do: you put a bucket full of water on the fire and bring it to the boil. Then you empty two or maybe three packets of tea into the boiling water and stir. Then add three whole tins of condensed milk. The tea boy would spoon some hot water into the tins and put them aside to cool, these were mine! While all this was going on, I went round collecting the tin mugs in a sack. I always brought my own china cup from home, I wasn't allowed near the tea bucket. The tea boy dipped my cup in the brew, the floating tea leaves congregating around a twig were deftly scooped out of the bucket.

Remembering the insides of the men's mugs I can quite understand why she gave me a spotless 'posh' china cup.

Unfortunately for my Mother, I was not like my Father, a typical let's not make a fuss Englishman. I had inherited my Mother's Celtic fire and determination. About mid-morning the foreman came over to see why I hadn't turned up for work, as the list and the bag were waiting.

'Don't just stand there Raymond, off you go.'

I didn't need telling twice. I don't know what was said on the doorstep, but from then on I had my meals sitting on our door step. The workmen would wave to me and I would wave back. Once eating on the step almost proved fatal, as one hot summer's day I was eating a bowl of rice pudding, when I fell asleep face down in the pudding and nearly drowned.

I had a friend nearby, Aubrey Honour. He was six and lived in what was left of a farm. Throughout the fringes of London, houses were springing up like mushrooms. During the twenties and thirties contractors, like my Dad, hauled building materials during the summer and coal throughout the winter.

I liked going up to the Honour's farm, there was so much to do up there. Aubrey's Dad had rigged a rope swing from one of the beams in the barn – it must have been a good twenty feet long. I sat in a car tyre, thinking that I would be safe clinging onto the tyre like grim death, missing the walls of the barn by inches. If my Mother had seen me she would have killed Aubrey.

After a little while I became more daring, launching from the stack of hay bales. One thing I didn't try was pig riding, tho' I must admit I was tempted. If I fell off, I would go home smelling of pig poo, consequently the Honour farm would be out of bounds. Aubrey would sweep all the pig poo into a corner, spread straw over the floor of the pen and then drop a couple of carrots or apples into the pen. The pigs would start pushing and shoving. Choosing his moment, Aubrey would leap into the pen grabbing a pig's right ear and swing his left leg over the pig's back, then, taking a firm grip of its left ear, away they would go. Not for long though as the noise would bring someone running from the house.

Aubrey's innocent, 'I was just feeding them!' didn't cut much ice.

'Well don't, I won't tell you again!'

Years later I helped to slaughter Uncle Stan's blackmarket pig. My Uncle Jack, who was a butcher by trade, did the technical bits. My job was to manoeuvre the tin bath to catch the blood and guts. I thought of Aubrey and his happy pigs, it helped take my mind off the job in hand. I did feel sorry for the pig, but I ate some of it just the same.

My why why's became more frequent when Mum told me that we were moving.

'Why?'

'Because the Vicar wants to knock down the cottages and the stables and build a new Church.'

'Why? He's already got a Church! Will I be going to Sunday school in the new Church?'

'No, it's too far away.'

'But I have got lots of friends at Sunday school.'

And on and on. I bet my Mother wished she hadn't told me that we were moving.

Sunday school had a lot to answer for. A doctor friend said that all second and subsequent children were conceived on Sunday afternoons!

We lived where the now new Holy Cross Church is situated, in Ferrymead Avenue in Greenford, just off the A40. There are two churches there now – the original and the much larger one built in 1943.

Our cottage was originally built for the Vicar's 'outdoor' staff. They were redundant now that he had a motor car. His driver doubled as a driver/butler, his wife was the housekeeper and they lived in two attic rooms in the Vicar's manse. The stables, which once held a wagonette and four horses, were ideal for my Father's haulage business.

The cottages, built for a couple of hundred pounds a long time ago, had paper thin walls, not soundproof. When my Mum and Dad were having full and frank discussions, usually about money, or rather the lack of it, their arguing kept me awake.

I would slide across the linoleum and listen at the top of the stairs. I dare not walk as the floorboards were very creaky. My Mother did most of the talking – she talked about margins and percentages, all Double Dutch to me and thinking about it now, I think she must have had a lot of inside information about my Father's competitors.

The biggest row was over what he was going to replace Tom with, another horse or a tipper truck?

After a long pause my Father said, 'I have been giving it a lot of thought and I have decided to sack one of the drivers. You complain that you find it difficult to find the men's wages every Friday. This will be one less.'

My Mother said something in Welsh, then, 'Harold you are enough to daunt a saint!'

I realised many years later that our inevitable slide into poverty began at that moment. If my Father had worked and left my Mother to run the business, I would have become a playboy and died young.

I don't know what the attraction was; perhaps she thought she was marrying the Wooster money. Unfortunately for her and fortunately for me, she married the wrong brother.

My Father got the best of the bargain. He married a clever educated woman who was not afraid of hard work. She came from a mining village known as Ammanford. Her Father rose to become manager of one of the local pits. His brother, Maerdy Jones, started work as the sole bread winner at the tender age of thirteen, his Father having been killed in a mining accident. He became one of the first Labour MPs. Whether this inspired her to better herself I don't know, but she sent off for a correspondence secretarial course. She went to Chapel twice on Sunday, not for the good of her soul, but to take the sermons down in shorthand. An uncle made a mock typewriter keyboard out of plywood – how many hours she spent getting up to speed I shall never know.

She managed to land a job in a solicitor's office, aged fourteen, better than shop work with its long hours, lifting and humping. The shorthand and typing course had paid off.

'Does your ambition know no bounds? At fourteen you have a job that many would die for, why go to London? That den of iniquity,' asked her Father.

'I don't know. All I know is that I can see my future here and I don't like what I see.'

My Grandfather decided if you can't beat 'em, join 'em. He had a friend send him the 'sits vac' pages of the London evening newspapers. My Mother wrote off for many jobs, some in shorthand. The replies were encouraging, tho' they invariably said, 'write again when you are eighteen'. Then, a couple his friend knew, at the Welsh Chapel in Harrow on the Hill, were looking for a nanny for their two pre-school children. They ran a hardware shop in Sudbury Hill. Oddly, the shop is still there selling more or less the same stuff.

My Grandfather took my Mother to Swansea and kitted her out summer and winter, so to speak. In return, a letter or postcard had to drop on his door mat every first of the month.

My Mother had landed on her feet, the shop owners were kind and the children well behaved. Not one to sit about and do nothing, she helped in the shop. Two years passed quickly, the children were about to start school.

Time to look around for another position – a pub in Wealdstone was advertising for a cook. She could cook.

The publican Mr Strawbridge said, 'I'm looking for someone a bit older, more experienced, it's hard work you know.'

'I know – how many for dinner?'

'Four. That's a coal fired range.'

'I have cooked on nothing else since I was a little girl. Now where is everything?'

She took an overall from the back of the door and hung her coat in its place.

'Well?'

'I like your nerve Miss Jones. What's your first name?'

'Gwendoline but everyone calls me Gwen.'

'Against my better judgement I shall leave you to get on with it. I hate being watched myself when I am working, any problems give me a shout – I shall be in the bar.'

'Sit up, dinner's ready.'

The table had been laid on a pure white tablecloth. She had ransacked the linen cupboard to find the best tablecloth. It was obvious they normally dined off the bare wood.

'Well?'

'When can you start?'

When and how my parents met I have no idea, my Father was somewhat of a snob, he didn't smoke Player's Navy Cut or Craven A, always Turkish Abdulla's. From his highly polished pointed toe shoes to his Fedora hat, he was very much a young man about town.

The Move

All I knew was that we were moving to Preston House near the White Hart pub, at the west end of Northolt.

Talking of moving, in those poverty stricken days, the bulk of the population was on the move. It was called 'doing a moonlight flit'. A coal man's flatbed trolley was ideal for the job. 'Saturday afternoon, five bob, okay?'

When the coal man arrived back at the yard that evening, 'Missis Wooster.'

'Yes.'

'Do the Smiths at forty-one Chestnut Avenue owe you for coal?'

'I'll just check. It's okay thank you.' Or, 'they owe nineteen and six.'

My Dad would be waiting in ambush on his bike; he usually got most of what he was owed.

The man was 'sacked' on the spot for moon lighting and told to walk back to the yard to collect his cards. My Dad gave the coal man a 'drink' for tipping him off.

Oh yes, the move, I was forgetting. The move was on a Saturday. I sat on the back step with Floss keeping out of the way. I travelled in the last wagon, sitting with Floss in a battered peddle car that my Mother had bought from a rag and bone man which Mr Hutt had got into working order. The yard dogs ran behind challenging the suburban dogs, who were safe behind their fences and gates, to come out and fight. Our yard dogs were thugs through and through and looked it and yet, I remember play fighting with them in the yard.

One day, when one of the drivers came out of the stable for a smoke (smoking was strictly forbidden in the stables), 'Here Bert come an' look at this,' said the smoker.

Bert contemplated the play fight for a while. Then said, ''Ee's the same in the stable. I told the gov'nor that boy's going to get kicked one of these days, you mark my words, but 'e never took no notice.'

My Father instructed me not to feed the dogs until we got to Preston House, no doubt they could smell the horse meat. The dogs were fed on raw horse meat and liver six days a week and starved on Wednesday. Bones were plentiful all through the week. I wonder what my Father's generation would make of the diet of modern dogs.

As soon as we arrived, the dogs were chained up. I was dying to explore, but the animals came first. Feed and water the dogs, water the horses and then up into the gloomy hay loft to refill the hay racks. Then it was our turn, corned beef sandwiches and apple pie, washed down with billy tea.

Preston House was huge, well I thought so, with large dusty echoing rooms. How many people had lived here I wondered? Listening to my parents at mealtimes, as my Grandmother would say 'little pigs have big ears.'

'The house was much too big; good servants were like gold dust and the rates of pay they demanded! Who needs stables in this day and age' and so on.

It's strange how memories long ago stuffed in the attic of the brain are dusted down and brought out into the light of day. Actions, over which we had no control, are like puffs of cloud heralding a storm to come. Ignore them at your peril! No doubt she could see what was coming!

Many years later we would discuss the past, or as I called it, raking the ashes. She enjoyed listening to my words of praise of her hard work and fortitude. Mostly, my sitting on her lap watching the soldiers in the fire, listening to her singing and telling stories. I think I must have been her dummy and Teddy rolled into one.

Where was I? Oh yes moving.

I had raced and chased all over the house and then I saw it! Through the landing window! A duck pond, complete with ducks!

I dashed down to the kitchen, where Mr Hutt and my parents were having a well-earned cup of tea.

'You must come and see what I have found!' I was jumping up and down with excitement.

'I've finished me tea,' Mr Hutt said, 'come on, let's see what you 'ave found.'

We were not gone long.

'E's found the duck pond!'

My Mother was out of the kitchen like a greyhound out of the traps.

My parents and Mr Hutt stood looking at the pond.

'You didn't say anything about a pond Harold.'

'I only looked at the stables.'

My Mother's tone was icy. 'If Mr Hutt cannot make that pond child proof by Wednesday, I'm off. Correction, we're off. Do you understand?'

Without waiting for a reply, she turned on her heel and left.

'Well guv, we're in a pickle an' no mistake.'

'She'll be over it by tomorrow.'

'No, she won't Guv. Look, let me 'av the trolley. I know where I can pick up some 'erdles and a lot of barbed wire. It's a bit rusty but it will do.'

'Where is this wire?'

'Why, Johnny Rocks's place, just down the road.'

'He was best man at my wedding Joe.'

'Should come cheap then?'

To cut a long story short, the pond was made safe, as safe as you can make a pond safe. When my Mother came to inspect their handy work, she said, 'Are you sure that Raymond won't be able to get through your barbed wire Mr Hutt?'

Mr Hutt took a deep puff on his pipe and exhaled, 'Why Missis Wooster, if the Germans didn't get through my barbed wire, I'm sure that your boy won't.'

My Father, not a humorous man, often told the story against my Mother.

Mr Green

If it wasn't one thing it was another. We had been in the new house little more than a week, when Floss came proudly trotting across the field which separated us from Mr Green's property, with a dead chicken clenched between her jaws. She reluctantly gave up her prize and while we were struggling I noticed blood on her flanks.

'She's been shot Mum! Look! There are four holes where the pellets went in – see.'

I picked up Floss and carried her out to the yard. Mr Hutt, who was busy in the tack room repairing harnesses, would know what to do.

'Look what Mr Green has done to my Floss!' I said, through floods of tears and sobs.

'Come outside in the light and let's 'ave a look.' He up-turned a bucket and sat me on it.

'Now, 'old 'er tight or she'll 'av me. Them pellets 'aven't gone in too far. Put yer arm round 'er body good an' tight. Wiv yer other 'and grab 'er muzzle good an 'ard. We'll 'av them pellets out in a trice.'

'Yes, Mr Hutt.'

Mr Hutt gripped his pipe between his teeth and took out the tool of all trades – his trusty clasp knife. He carefully wiped the blade on his trousers – that blade might cut up his lunch or clean a horse's hoof. Now, it was going to dig pellets out of Floss's bottom.

Floss whimpered and I am sure could have broken free from me at any time. When the last pellet popped out Mr Hutt dabbed Stockholm tar on the wounds.

'Right, you 'ave got a new dog, a spotty dog.'

'Thank you, Mr Hutt.'

'Don't thank me boy. Now you listen to me. When you see's Mr Green next time, you say thank you for not killin' my Floss, Mr Green.'

I mumbled something whilst looking at his feet.

'No no, not like that! Stand up straight. 'Ead up, look me in the eye. Louder – that's more like it. Now go and walk round the pond and practice, then come back so's I knows that you've got it right. Now off you go and take the dog with you, I've got work to do.'

I am forever grateful to Mr Hutt for that first lesson in what an American called 'people skills'. Many, many years later, I once overheard my kindly Uncle Stan say to my Father, 'Young Raymond is a bolshie little sod, don't you think so Harold?'

'Why do you say that?'

'Oh, the way he looks at you when he's talking to you.' My Father gave a deep sigh, 'I know what you mean – he gets it from his Mother.'

Many years later an American complimented me on my 'people skills'. I didn't get it from my Mother, she polished what Mr Hutt had begun.

Mr Green, my Mother was sure, didn't want his rather chewed up chicken back, so we had it for dinner and very nice it was too. The next day it was planned that my Mother and I would go to Mr Green's house with a duck as a peace offering, but first catch your duck.

I had been appointed duck herd. It was my job to let the ducks out in the morning from their 'duck shed'. Not a problem – the moment I opened the shed door Floss would chase them to the pond, the highlight of her day. Evening also not a problem. I only had to rattle their feed tin and they would come running. It had been decided that a pure white duck would be THE duck. Floss and I slipped into the shed watched by my Mother and Mr Hutt, who said he wouldn't have missed it for worlds. The noise! Floss and I managed to pin the right duck into one of the corners. I had taken an old tarp in with me, together with four house bricks to hold it down. The ducks were cowering in the back of the shed. Just as I had the white duck, Floss panicked the others and in the melee I lost the duck. So I chucked Floss out and started again. Instead of racing and chasing about, I walked slowly, creeping up on Whitey. I grabbed her beak with my left hand, my right arm holding her wings tight against her body and my right hand grasping her feet. Mr Hutt took the duck, coming to my rescue, as it was all I could do to hold it.

Mr Hutt put the protesting duck into a horse's nose bag and secured it, that was the easy bit. I was made presentable, my Mother put on her best coat and off we went to Mr Green's house.

At three years old I had no idea of the sleazy world of grown-ups. The Greens were not married! They were living in sin! She had been a Land Army girl during the 14/18 war and they had fallen in love and decided to live together. It was a very civilised arrangement, his wife continued to live in the house and in the meantime, he had a 'kit' home built in a corner of the large acreage he owned. It would be nice if they had lived happily ever after, but no, she was shunned as a 'fallen woman'. As we walked through the Express Dairy yard my Mother said, 'Don't let me down, will you?'

I had been rehearsing my 'Thank you, Mr Green' speech in my head all the way there.

My Mother placed the nose bag in front of the door and stood behind me. I knocked on the door and after what seemed like an age, Mr Green answered the door.

I doffed my cap and began, 'Good morning, Mr Green.'

'Jean, here a minute.' A lady came to the door drying her hands on a towel.

'Yes, what is it?'

'Tell this lady what you just told me. Your name?'

'Raymond, Raymond Wooster.' I repeated my spiel.

'And what's in the nose bag?'

A muffled quack answered her query. My Mother explained the reason for our visit.

'Mrs Wooster, your coat!'

'Duck mess I'm afraid, it will clean off.'

'Oh no it won't, take your coat off and bring it in. I've just put the kettle on.'

Mr Green and I took the duck to the fowl coop where he showed me the mended fence where Floss had got in.

'My fault, should have checked it. Floss only killed one, if she was a fox she would have killed the lot, so thank Floss for me. That tea should be on the table by now old son and some homemade cakes.'

What a result, lonely 'Mrs Green' has a friend and so has my Mum and I. The coat, as good as new, was delivered by the Advance Laundry man.

Croxstan's Seven Sisters Riding School

I had become curious about the riding school after hearing my parents talking about the Croxstans at the table.

I decided to pay them a visit. I missed the builders and the tea boy, not to mention Aubrey Honor. My Mother had done everything she could to keep me away from the farm, short of an outright ban, which would be counterproductive.

One cold sunny day, when I was nearly five years old, I set out for the riding school which was about a ten-minute walk from Preston House. I didn't walk into the yard, that would be rude. Instead I stood looking through the iron railings and sure enough a young woman approached me, 'Are you lost little boy, where is your Mummy?'

'My Mummy is at home,' I pointed, 'down there.'

'Would you like a ride on my pony? I am going to get her reshod at the farrier's. On the way you can show me where you live. Come along in – don't be nervous. I will introduce you to the pony before you ride her.'

She put her hand into her britches' pocket and withdrew some sugar lumps and gave them to me. She noticed that I held my hand flat and remarked that I knew how to feed horses without losing my fingers. She led the pony to the mounting block – this was much better than being handed up. With my Father's horses I sat on the horse's neck taking two hands' full of mane and clinging on for dear life as it was a long way down. Whereas with the pony I could sit back holding the reins like a proper rider, even though I didn't have a saddle.

Ann, for that was her name, knocked on the front door. My Mother opened it and before Ann could speak, I announced that, 'We are going to the farrier's to have the pony shod.' [Cocky little sod!]. Ann and my Mother stood talking for what seemed an age, until Ann noticed that the pony was nibbling the roses. I pulled as hard as I could on the reins but the pony would have none of it. As we moved off, I waved to my Mother. She replied with a shaking fist. Not very nice I thought, anyway, I will worry about that later. I had never been in a farrier's workshop before, the sound of metal on metal, the stench as red hot metal was pressed against the horse's hoof.

I must have driven Ann mad with my incessant 'whys.' On the contrary, she seemed to enjoy my Q and A sessions and pointed out things that I hadn't asked about.

'When's your birthday, sonny?' the farrier asked.

'January, Sir.'

'Here's a birthday present for you, it's a bit late but better late than never eh? I forgot to ask your age.'

'I'm four, Sir.'

The farrier opened a cupboard and took out a shiny black horseshoe. 'Nail it to your front door with the round bit at the bottom and it will bring you good luck, the other way up an' all your luck will run out.'

'Thank you, Sir, thank you.' I stammered and clutched the horseshoe to my chest. Another little job for Mr Hutt.

'You have made a little boy very happy,' said a smiling Ann.

'Oh it's nothin',' he waved a hand, 'I keeps a few in the cupboard for them as I take's a shine to.'

Shaving the Cat

I was sat on an upturned bucket in the hay shed watching the rain come down and the dogs were doing what they liked best – sleeping. I had spent an hour play fighting with them, until they became bored and flopped out in the hay. I do wish we were back in Greenford. There I could look forward to Aubrey Honour coming home from school with some of his friends. One of my Mother's favourite sayings was, 'The Devil makes work for idle hands.' What it meant I had no idea.

Sitting on the bucket looking at the supine dogs, the Devil spoke to me.

I had been fascinated watching Dad shaving. It was quite a ritual. I would climb into the bath and sit on the rim as he created a foamy beard, then with deft strokes, removed it. All this was done in total silence, not a 'why' escaped my lips. The more I thought about it the more I liked the idea, no sooner said than done.

I nipped indoors, collected the oilskin bag with my Dad's shaving tackle in it, topped up the mug from the horse trough and in no time at all, the brush whisked up a nice foam.

The next question, which dog?

Ben or Buster, our yard dogs? Then again, Floss the house dog had a very soft coat.

Ben was lying stretched out, his head between his front legs, quite relaxed, he quite enjoyed having his spine soaped. However, I had hardly shaved an inch when Ben leapt to his feet and bolted for the sanctuary of his kennel. Buster raised his head, looked round and went back to sleep. Ben's sudden movement resulted in me sustaining several cuts on my left fingers, as my Mother said, 'Thank God for safety razors.'

Like Ben, Buster enjoyed the soaping but not the shaving. He was half awake and made an even faster getaway. When I looked round for Floss, she was slinking out of the hay shed and lost no time scratching at the kitchen door to be let in.

I wound my handkerchief around my left hand. If I could stop the bleeding before lunch I might get away with it.

Then … what should come into the hay shed – one of the semi feral cats. I had made friends with all the cats. My Dad gave orders that the cats were not to be fed, they should hunt for their food. But there, what's a bit of horse meat between friends.

To cut a long story short, I got within an inch of her tail when she exploded into a ball of furry fury. There would be no explaining away the scratches on both my arms or the pain that I was in. We hadn't been in the house very long, my parents had no idea where the nearest doctor's surgery was. Then Mother remembered that Mrs Green had been a VAD nurse after she left the Land Army. We ran across the field, they took the situation in immediately. Mrs Green wrapped a towel round each arm, meanwhile Mr Green brought his car round and we all piled in.

On the way, Mr Green asked, 'What happened?'

I told the truth, I never lied to my Mother, not because I was a goody goody, it was pointless. She always got to the truth and the truthful journey was painless.

When I got to Ben bolting to his kennel, Mr Green began to laugh. By the time I got to the exploding furry fury, everyone was laughing, even me, through my pain. The doctor was rather puzzled by three adults and a four year old in obvious pain, laughing.

'Tell the doctor what happened,' Mr Green said.

I was quite pleased at the grown-ups' response to my story that is until the doctor stuck a needle into my arm.

My Mother asked the doctor if she could pay him on Friday, these were the days before the NHS.

'Mr Green and I enjoyed your son's story so much we have agreed to split the bill between us. There are very few laughs in medicine and Mr Green can't wait to tell the story over dinner at the lodge.'

Their kindness reduced my Mother to tears. Where she was going to get the money by Friday was any one's guess. It would have had to be paid off a few shillings a week.

By the time my Father came home the humour had gone out of the story. He immediately went across to Mr Green's house to thank him for his help, promising to deliver half a ton of anthracite on Thursday.

For the next week or so I was on my best behaviour. I didn't need reminding to do my chores, like filling the hay racks. I also found a way to ingratiate myself with my Mother, she hated the duck pond but adored the ducks. The ducks were kept in a shed overnight safe from foxes. I noticed that the dirt floor had become a mix of mud and duck poo and there were several sheds in various states of dereliction. The best one had a cement floor easy to keep clean, also I didn't have to paddle through all that muck to collect the eggs then wash my Wellingtons under the tap every time.

I was busting to tell her about the new duck house, how I managed to keep it a secret I don't know, but I did.

'Raymond, I have just been down to the duck shed for some eggs and the nest boxes have gone. I am sure that Mr Hutt hasn't moved them.'

'Oh I forgot to tell you [rotten little liar!], they are in a different shed now, would you like to see it?'

When she saw the newly swept floor and the nest boxes with eggs in them just inside the door, she was overwhelmed, then suspicious.

'Are you sure that Mr Hutt didn't do all this?'

'E done it all his self, I watched. All I did was give 'im a 'and with the nest boxes.'

To think that I had managed to keep the new duck shed a secret for three whole days!

A few weeks later we had a hard frost, the edges of the pond had a few inches of ice. As Mr Hutt said to my Dad, 'Let's 'ope this is as cold as it gets 'arold. Where are them ducks? I left the shed door open. Raymond's gone indoors for the feed tin, that'll bring 'em.'

Seeing the duck shed door open I had assumed they were down at the pond. The fox! No, if the fox had got them there would be feathers everywhere. I rattled the feed tin. A loud quacking came from the shed and the ducks came out shuffling and limping. Dad and Mr Hutt had joined me at the shed. They began laughing which brought the men out from the stable who also began to laugh.

'What are they laughing at Dad?'

When my father got himself together, he explained that the cold concrete had locked their legs and they couldn't walk. I was mortified. What with the shaving business now this, tears began to flow. Dad picked me up.

'Don't cry, they'll be alright when they warm up. Now, go with Mr Hutt to the hay shed and get a truss of straw. Mr Hutt will show you what to do with it. I must be off to work. Now don't let the ducks see you crying. Spread the straw on the floor of the duck shed and the ducks will love you.'

That evening the ducks snuggled down in the straw, at last I had done something right.

'May I go up to the riding school Mummy,' I said casually and before she could answer, there was a knock at the door and I answered it. Who should it be but Ann?

'I am taking one of the hunters to the farrier's to have some studs fitted to her shoes, just in case we get some black ice. I thought Raymond might like to come with me? And Dad asked if you would mind if he came to tea? It would be nice to have another man at the table for a change.'

How I kept silent I don't know. On reflection I think my Mother was glad to see the back of me for a few hours. Her 'Oh go on then, but mind you behave yourself,' was music to my ears.

Giving my Mother a quick hug I was out of the door and waiting for a leg up onto the hunter. It seemed a long wait as Ann and my Mother stood chatting, I fed the hunter a few roses and that seemed to do the trick. Sitting high up on the hunter I was as proud as a cockerel on a dung hill. I waved and my Mother waved back, not her fist this time.

Over tea I was grilled about the shaving episode. I was close to tears most of the time – not the shaving, the remorse. I had cost my parents money they could ill afford and I was well aware of the problems they faced. Their conversations or rows were always about money or lack of it, the first word that I learned to spell was R E N T.

Many years later, discussing my relationship with the Greens and the Croxtans, my Mother explained that I was the child the Greens never had, also my apology for Floss stealing the chicken captivated them. As to the Croxtan's seven girls, I was the son he never had. I pointed out that they had lots of nephews. To quote Mr Hutt, 'bleedin' posh 'ooligans, every one of 'em.'

'So, I wasn't a moment's worry to my white haired young Mother,' I said.

As she got up to make the coffee she took a swing at me, as she often said, 'I was never too old to get a clip round the ear.'

Just as I was settling down and making new friends, there was talk of moving again. I tried not to show any interest in the conversations, few of which were held in my hearing, however, I heard enough to unsettle me. I began to fantasize about what I would do when I grew up. I would have a business and make lots of money which would stop all these rows and constant moving.

My Mother sensing my unease talked about me starting school next year, 'Won't it be wonderful?' she said. Getting no response from me she said, 'What's the matter?'

'Nothing.'

'But you're always talking about going to school.'

'I know.'

And so on and so on until I said, 'Well – I haven't filled the hay racks.'

That let my Mother off the hook, the more we talked the worse it became, she stayed off the subject until crunch time.

The Greens and the Croxtans noticed that I wasn't my usual chatty self and asked if anything was the matter? To which I replied, 'No, no I am fine.' What else could I say? Luckily I had Floss, who I am sure picked up on my state of mind and sat across my lap to be fussed at every opportunity.

In the early spring, weather willing, Mr Hutt and I took two wagon loads of carthorse harnesses down to Glebe farm. Mrs Rocks always treated us to a meal despite Mr Hutt's protestations. Floss always stayed sitting on the box, I think she was wary of their yard dogs, fortunately I had a bone for her to gnaw on.

Normally I would be full of questions – 'Was my Dad going to sell his horses and buy a lorry? Why were we taking all these harnesses to Glebe farm?'

Mr Hutt tried to strike up a conversation only to be met with silence, probably just as well. What I wanted him to say would be a lie, if he told me the truth he knew what the result would be, so silence was the best policy.

Two Sundays later my Dad took two horses down to Glebe farm. On Monday two drivers did not turn up for work.

'Where are we going to next Mummy?'

'Not far. You know Northolt Station? Our new house is about as far from the station as the Croxtans are from here.'

'Is Mr Hutt coming with us Mummy?'

'No Cariad (Welsh for darling/sweetheart), but Daddy is going to take him on again when business picks up.'

A fib – a black fib. She knew it and so did I.

'Why didn't Mr Hutt say goodbye? Not very kind to leave without saying goodbye.'

'He was to upset Cariad but he gave me this for you.'

She handed me his clasp knife.

'He told me to tell you to keep it safe until you are a boy scout.'

To say that I was inconsolable was the understatement of the year. I was unable to say goodbye to the Croxtans and Mr and Mrs Green. Instead Mam wrote a letter to each of them which Floss and I slipped through their letter boxes after dark.

The next morning there were two letters on the door mat, one from Ann Croxtan and the other from Mr and Mrs Green.

When we had settled into our new house Mr Croxtan would pick me up on Friday in his car. In his car!!! I would spend the weekend with them and Mr Green would bring me home on Sunday evening. I had no idea what their real motives were.

The last thing my pregnant Mother needed was a weepy child moping about the place. I didn't know that she was expecting my sister Jean. Such topics were very much hush hush, babies just appeared. One day I was an only child and the next day I had a sister. That event was several months down the track.

Meanwhile, I enjoyed my weekends 'working' in the stables. I could shovel and sweep but not wheel a barrow. The grown-ups were surprised at the rapport I had with the dogs and the horses. Leading one of the big hunters out to the water trough and the tack room one day, I overheard one of the riders say to another, 'Look at that whippersnapper – literally got that horse eating out of his hand.'

I didn't take Floss with me but she always gave me a warm welcome when I came home, which made me feel guilty.

The 'new' house had once been a farmhouse on the corner of Eastcote Lane and Mandeville Road, now a petrol station, with stabling for two horses. The house had well water as well as mains water. I didn't waste any time trying out the pump handle – pumping the handle vigorously produced a gratifying gush of water. Dad took the handle off!

'Don't drink this water as we don't know where it's come from. Use the tap.'

I suppose the novelty of the pump handle would have soon worn off.

My Mother, now that we were on a bus route, invited my three posh Aunts over for afternoon tea, why I don't know, for me it was absolute torture. After a while, usually after they had pumped me dry and the home-made cakes were eaten, I would ask, 'May I go to Bobby Buckland's house Mummy?'

Unfortunately, such was my haste, that as I got down from the table I broke wind, not discreetly, but worthy of one of my Father's horses. I looked at my Mother and she looked at me.

'I did say pardon Mummy, but it still smells.'

Like Yorick, I had unwittingly set the table on a roar. I didn't hang about. I fled. When I got home that evening nothing was said. However, until my last Aunt drew her last breath, when we met they would always inquire, 'Does it still smell, Raymond?'

Starting School

School, at last! The headmistress was reluctant to admit me as I was too young. I was five in January and would have to wait till August. My Mother begged and pleaded but to no avail. Then she played her ace! She produced a book from her handbag. *Mother See Kitty*.

'He can read,' and handed the book to me. We had been practising for weeks with several books, this was my best book. I read from cover to cover with one or two stumbles, I could see that the headmistress was most impressed.

'Do you know your colours?'

I reeled them off.

'Numbers?'

When I got to fifteen, she stopped me.

'I have to admit, Mrs Wooster, that I am impressed. If only more parents took an interest in their children's education instead of leaving it all to us.'

'Where I come from education is revered,' my Mother replied. 'His sister was born on the 21st of September. How would it be if a scatty mother put a nine, instead of a one?'

The head tore up the form that my Mother had just completed and took out a fresh one.

'I have to pop to the staff room for a few minutes. Could you fill in this form whilst I am gone, Mrs Wooster?'

'Certainly.'

And that is how my Mother managed to shift one burden from her shoulders. As she told me many years later it was not without a certain poignancy. When she took me to school for the first time and settled me at my desk, I dismissed her with a wave of the hand and, 'You can go now Mum.' She was not allowed to take me to school or collect me. I came and went with my friends.

Talking of friends, they lived in Eastcote Lane and Moat Farm Road. Moat Farm Road was originally a road of middle class bungalows with a field of about three acres at the end.

I had wide circle of friends, I don't know who led who astray. There were plenty of orchards in Northolt and we knew which ones grew the sweetest juiciest fruits.

The owners knew who we were, yet they never complained to our parents, of course 'scrumping' was not without its hazards, a clip around the ear, barbed wire along the top of the fence, not a problem – a thick jacket thrown over the wire protected you from the worst of the barbs.

Dogs were a real hazard. My Mother noticed some red marks on my ankles. 'What are those marks.'

'Oh,' I said nonchalantly, 'I was playing with Bobby Buck-lands' dog.'

'Well don't, you will get lock jaw.'

'Yes Mum.'

Explaining away a bag of fruit wasn't difficult. 'John Smith's dad gave it to me.'

With no sweets to be had we craved something sweet, also there was what is known today as the adrenalin rush.

One day we were over the park, when John Fry's brother came over to tell us that old Froman had gone out with his dog. Now old Froman grew THE most delectable plums and pears behind a high fence. The fence was not a major problem to us boys. Froman had an even stronger line of defence, his dog!!

With Froman and his dog out of the way we were over the fence in a trice. Fortunately John Fry's brother had brought several sandbags with him. I was up the pear tree like a rat up a drainpipe, the juiciest pears grew at the top of the tree. My sandbag, now three quarters full I decided to move to another part of the tree when Froman's dog burst out of the kitchen door like Mick The Miller out of the traps.

I froze, for the others it was every boy for himself, they cleared the fence not before the dog got some nips in first, judging by the yelps. The grass was strewn with abandoned overflowing sandbags. Having put the boys to flight, the dog turned its attention to my tree. He began jumping up the tree trunk barking in 'dogie': 'he's up there, you old fool, can't you see him?'

Fortunately Old Froman couldn't tell the boy from the tree. He picked up one of the sacks and made his way to the kitchen door. The thwarted dog went loopy. Froman swung at the dog with his stick, which the dog avoided with ease – much practice I suppose.

Having got rid of two problems, I was faced with a much worse one. I was busting for a pee, a dog bite is a badge of honour, to pee your pants out of fear, well!

I won't keep you in suspense any longer, I made it just in time. Without doubt that was the best pee I ever had, bar none.

Discussing what went wrong we decided we were too greedy, half a sack would be plenty, how would we explain a whole sack away? 'Mrs Smith gave me a dozen apples.' Yes, yes much more believable.

Thinking about it, I decided that if I knocked on his door, doffed my cap, put on my gentleman Jim manner, 'Mr Froman, Sir, may I have some of your wind falls for my Mother?'

'Certainly my boy, I got a sack, go round the back.'

He handed me the sack. I knew the sack, an old friend.

'Would you like me to pick some for you Mr Froman, Sir.'

'Indeed I would my boy, indeed I would.'

He handed me another sack. This sack I picked from the trees, the best.

All in my sack were wind falls, I had to convince my mother.

Mr Froman's, 'come again my boy, come again,' was music to my ears. I cannot say the same of the dog, it never stopped barking.

The next day I took two hot pies round to Mr Froman, which proved my Mother's maxim: 'You catch more flies with honey than you do with vinegar.'

With a free, plentiful supply of fruit, scrumping lost its excitement and thrills.

The council decided to build a small estate of houses to accommodate families from a slum clearance area in London. This did not enhance the value of the bungalows. We were hard up, but none the less, we did eat well. When the 'Council House Kids' called for me, my Mother would cut a 'doorstep' off a loaf and coated it with a liberal dollop of jam and gave it to them. When I asked 'Why?', she explained that the 'doorstep' was probably their breakfast. Poverty in those days was real, not relative.

When we moved to the corner house with just one horse, it didn't take me long to muck out and fill the hay rack. Then it was over to the park or wherever with my friends. This part of the village with its school was more highly populated, although my Mother said, 'that there were so few men in the village, they had to take it in turns to be the village idiot.'

Most of the boys were a year or two older than me. I had an unfair advantage. Once, I had taken them up to the park entrance on Blaze's back two at a time. I or rather Blaze, of course, was the flavour of the month. The fee – carrots or a potato or two. I was very surprised that my Dad let me give my friends rides, but I always had to wait until she had eaten and drunk her fill. Sometimes, if Dad's dinner wasn't ready, he would sit on the back steps, smoking a cigarette and watch the fun.

One of the benefits of free rides was the grooming. My friends loved to curry comb the horse. I have forgotten her name, but she was chestnut with a white diamond blaze between her eyes, so let's call her Blaze. Horses being herd animals did not like to be alone. Blaze was no exception. Imagine, trudging around all day pulling a coal cart often wet and cold. The yard dogs now slept on a sack filled with hay under Blaze's manger.

Fronting onto Mandeville Road was a field of about an acre – there was talk of a cinema being built on it. It was surrounded by a high chain link fence, too high for people to chuck rubbish over, the grass about knee high, ideal for my plan.

The entrance was through a padlocked steel gate. I examined the lock and to my surprise it flopped open. It had been forced at some time and now it was bluffing.

There were a few dusty old locks in a draw in the kitchen each with a least one key. A few drops of oil and I had what I wanted.

My Father finished early that evening, shut Blaze out and hung her harness on the baily.

'Leave her to me Dad.'

A drink and then a handful of pig nuts, a handful?

I am sure she looked at me quizzically.

Headstall on, out of our gate and across the lane into the field.

Blaze stood in the long grass for a few seconds and then took off like a rocket with Floss hard on her heels.

I called Floss back when Blaze started to roll and squirm, she was behaving like a young colt. I was almost in tears when a voice said, 'and what's your game?'

I couldn't answer for a while, but then I explained.

His hand on my shoulder, and 'you did well' was praise indeed.

'Wait here while I go for a bucket of cattle cake, I am sure that your Mother would like to see this.'

We left her grazing until it got dark.

I rattled the bucket, 'Come on, come on.'

Like a reluctant child she ambled across the field.

Come rain, hail or shine, she spent every evening and Sundays in the field. No one queried the horse in the field, what could be more natural than a horse in a field?

Passers by would feed her crusts, carrots and other tit bits. Result? One very happy horse.

Many of my friends had pet dogs or cats, but a horse! Little did they know how much hard work it entailed.

Two of my friends offered to help and I let them fill the hay racks. They finished up chucking hay about the loft.

As my Dad said, 'A boy is a boy, two boys is half a boy, three boys isn't a boy at all. Send your friends home, then clear up this mess.'

To my surprise I found that the girls worked best, what they lacked in physical strength they more than made up for in effort. Also they fell in love with Blaze. It took me a while to overcome their fear, after all they were high up above the ground. I put a horse blanket on Blaze and secured it with two belly bands. All three could ride at the same time.

My Mother was rather anxious, in case one or all of them came a cropper, she was reassured when I expressed the same fears to the girls.

'Fear not Raymond,' one of the girls said, 'Mummy has watched several times.'

'I haven't seen her.'

'That's because she stands by the Police box, not with all the others next to the fence. If we are any good our Daddies will pay for proper riding lessons.'

They were two or three years older than me and went to a private school in Harrow. I had no idea where they lived – probably Alderney Gardens, judging by their posh accents.

Then the inevitable happened, the Daddies decided to pay for riding lessons at the Seven Sister's Riding School on my recommendation. The next time I visited the Croxtans they thanked me for the three new riders and they had recommended others from their school.

When they dropped me of at the corner house Mr Croxtan handed me an envelope.

'Here you are old son, start a Post Office savings account.'

'Thank you, Mr Croxtan Sir,' and I ran in doors clutching the envelope.

'Mum! Mum! Look what Mr Croxtan gave me!'

'Well don't stand there waving it about like a flag, open it.'

I took a knife from the cutlery draw and began to fumble.

'You do it please Mum as I might tear something.'

We sat at the table, me all excited, she cool and deliberately extracted a letter which she opened and out dropped a Postal Order.

My aunt beckoned and put her finger to her lips. I had never seen a new baby before, she was all red and wrinkly and the noise, it didn't seem to bother my Mother in the least. I kissed my Mother and the baby.

'I will wait on the back step for Dad and tell him when he comes home.'

As I sat on the step I remembered how my Mother would take a nap in the afternoon, how grateful she was when I helped her lift the heavy washing out of the boiler, turning the mangle was no effort for me, I quite enjoyed it. Two days later the Beltons left for home. I would miss my uncle and aunt but not Billy. Little did I know that in a few years Jean and I would be living with them as evacuees from the bombing.

'Why did the ambulance take Jean away Mummy?'

'Because she is very ill Cariad. I don't know what is the matter but the hospital will make her better.'

It was pneumonia and croup. Not a surprise to my Mother, the corner house was a perishing cold hole. I think my Mother summed it up with 'the wind blows you in and the draught blows you out.'

Jean was not in Harrow or Ealing hospitals but Isleworth, but then as she said, 'beggars can't be choosers.'

We were allowed one visit. I can still see her pale face in the oxygen tent, the latest piece of technology, without it she would have died.

While Jean was in hospital two events changed everything.

There were the usual rows, but my Mother seldom raised her voice now.

On the Move Again

'We are off – you do what you like,' repeated over and over again. Then our landlord Mr Saich increased the rent, if my Mother's ultimatum didn't do the trick, then the rent hike was the last straw.

While Jean was in hospital my Mother had found a two up two down mid-terraced house – number 28 Mandeville Road, about a hundred yards from the corner house. I wouldn't have to change schools or friends.

My Father did not give up easily. He had found a cottage with a stable but my Mother was having none of it. If push came to shove my Welsh grandparents would take us in.

As she said, 'she had had it up to here with bloody horses.'

We moved into 28 just before the next month's rent was due.

Then, irony of ironies. Within two weeks of us moving out, a gypsy family squatted in the house, the Staffords.

Saich didn't get a penny rent out of them even tho' they prospered for many years or I should say the pub (the Plough) across the way did. Stafford had a stationary engine driving a huge circular saw. His wife and two sons spent every spare minute of their time cutting up logs until the NSPCC put a stop to it. My Father loaded up the trolley and took all his harness and stuff down to the Glebe Farm. I was very sad to see Blaze go but it was nice while it lasted. Dad commuted on his old rattle trap bike.

1938 – Things were looking up. My Mother had got a job at a recently built posh public house – The TARGET. It didn't have a (spit and saw dust) public bar, just two bars, saloon and private. Mother was the speciality cook whatever that was. If she could see it now! Gone are the Rolls, Bentleys and Daimlers. Now it's a bloody McDonald's.

She worked from 11 a.m. until 3 p.m. Saturdays and Sundays.

Jean was looked after by a neighbour, Mrs Davey, who had two little girls of her own. Jean's pram went to work with her and was parked in the garage next to the owner's S.S. Jaguar which I lusted after. The pram carried home four containers, three full of leavings for the chickens and rabbits as the previous occupants of 28 had left a chicken run and six rabbit hutches behind when they left in a hurry. My Mother was broke of course; however, I had Mr Green's money in the Post Office and my errand sock in the draw upstairs. That might buy a rabbit.

Where to buy the chickens and rabbits? We hadn't a clue.

'I will be late home tonight Mum, I'm going round to John Cracknell's house on the way home,' I lied.

'Don't be late.'

I couldn't wait for 3.30 p.m., then up Church Road, running and jogging, suppose the Greens were out? Perhaps Mr Croxtan would advise me. All these what ifs ran through my head, as my Mother would say 'worrying never solved anything.'

I waited in the Express Dairy yard (where Todd Doors, Church Road, is now) while I got my breath back. Over a cup of tea and a cake I explained our problem.

'What you want young Raymond is a flock of a dozen point of lays and a cockerel so that you can add to the flock as you go.'

He didn't say anything about the rabbits apart from, 'I must Lysol the hutches and the chicken run before I sold them.'

I didn't tell him that I had already done it, the hutches and the run were disgusting.

It didn't take long for me to realise that he was talking about how he would go about it not me. I had gone there with such high hopes only to have them dashed, ah well I must have another think.

'Time I was running you home,' he glanced at his watch, 'Your Mother will think you have run away to sea, oh and by the way, wear some old clobber on Friday. We have got a dirty job on'.

'Thank you Mr Green for your advice. I will tell Mum.'

With that I jumped out of the car and ran down our back alley.

Friday came and I waited on the corner, early as usual, I never kept them waiting. I was surprised when, instead of a car, a horse box pulled up with Mr Croxtan at the wheel and Mr Green in the passenger seat. Mr Green got out and I scrambled in on top of the engine cowling, my favourite spot. The cowling was pretty hot so I sat on my bag with my 'dirty jobs' clobber in it. I had hoped I would see some of my friends, or rather they would see me, no such luck.

Conversation was impossible, fortunately I was not in a chatty mood, preoccupied with chickens and rabbits or rather a lack of them.

Out along the Western Avenue towards Beaconsfield down a lane, or rather a leafy tunnel, Mr Green jumped down and opened a five barred gate. A man came out of a shed which seemed miles long. Mr Croxtan backed up the horse box to the door of the shed, naturally I was desperate to see what was in the shed.

'Put your working clobber on Raymond, there's work to be done.'

'Too late,' the moment Mr Green was out of the cab I was changed.

The side ramp was let down and pigeon baskets were passed from hand to hand and then carried to the huge shed. The man in charge opened the door. The noise! The stench!

There on the floor were thirteen chickens and one cockerel; the rabbits were in individual sacks which wriggled and squirmed.

The chickens lay passively, apart from the occasional flutter of wings, their legs bound with string tied in a neat bow.

We tenderly placed the birds three in a basket, the cockerel in a basket on his own.

'Tied up or not, those spurs could do frightful damage,' Mr Green said, 'lethal old chap.'

Mr Croxtan concurred. I was fascinated listening to them chatting to one another, not a bit like the men who worked for my Dad. The cockerel's spurs were fitted with leather 'gloves'.

'Just in case,' the man from the shed said.

'Jump up on your perch young Raymond,' Mr Green said, 'we are going into the office, won't be long.'

It was an opportunity not to be missed! I was up in the driver's seat with a firm grasp of the steering wheel making appropriate noises.

'E wants a watchin' guvner 'e does. Few years from now 'e will pinch a red 'ot stove and then come back for the smoke.'

I had no idea what they were laughing at, and I didn't care.

On the way home they carried on a shouted conversation, I am sure that my Mum and I featured in it, so what?

I was turning the steering wheel and changing gear in my head, the term hadn't been invented then, but I was a petrol head.

When we arrived there was so much to do. Mr Croxtan and Mr Green trundled the feed bins down to the empty shed, all of my Dad's stuff was down at the farm.

It came as more of a surprise to my Mother, who did the only thing she could – put the kettle on, take some freshly baked cakes from the oven and arrange the table and chairs in our back kitchen for her unexpected guests.

'I suppose that you are wondering what all the kerfuffle is about Mrs Wooster?'

'What on earth gives you that impression Mr Green?' she said without a flicker of a smile. 'Help yourselves to whatever you fancy.'

'Well,' said Mr Green, 'Mr Croxtan and I have been thinking of keeping chickens for quite some time now but he hasn't got the time and I haven't got the space. Now if we supplied the livestock and you took care of them in return, all we want is a plump chicken cooked as only you know how for our occasional dinner parties.' Then as an afterthought he said, 'With war on the horizon don't you think it would be sensible to have a source of meat and eggs, instead of relying on the black market.

'You are a forward planer Mr Green. I am sure Raymond and I will be able to run the farm but we must be able to make it secure. What do you think Mr Croxtan?'

'I will put it in hand tomorrow, trust a woman to think of the obvious.'

The following day, Sunday, a flatbed lorry backed into the alley, on board a kennel containing Buster. Our neighbour was on hand to give Dad and the driver a hand off with it.

We had spent Saturday incorporating half of his garden into ours. His garden had a huge elm tree growing in the top corner inhabited by a pair of owls which flew silently every night to their hunting ground in the local churchyard. The massive tree roots rendered number 28 and 30's gardens useless for anything in the crop line. My Mother had agreed to pay half a dozen eggs every first of the month rent for the plot, a bargain when the egg ration was one egg per week per person.

Buster was an added bonus, when the blackout was enforced, Buster's WOOF was a great comfort to those living around us. Buster wasn't chained up but had the run of both gardens as had the chickens. I don't know why but the cockerel and my Mother were never the best of friends.

One day my Mother stormed into the kitchen.

'That's it! I'm going to kill that bloody bird, you see if I don't!' she said grabbing a frying pan off the shelf.

'Must see this,' my Dad said, as he watched the dance of death.

The bird lunged, my Mum side stepped and caught the bird an almighty blow, or I should say 'boing'. The bird staggered and collapsed in a heap of feathers.

'Chicken for dinner next Sunday,' my Dad said as he picked up his newspaper. Dad was wrong, the bird recovered.

As my Mother said, 'violence works.' The cockerel kept a respectful distance from then on.

1939

Gas

Gas mask drill at school and over the park. The gas van would arrive and we children, six at a time, gas masks on, entered the van with two adults accompanying us, to ensure that our masks were correctly fitted. I was complimented on the tin of Vaseline I carried in my mask. The Vaseline ensured a gas tight fit. A tip from my kindly Uncle George who had fought the Turks at Gallipoli at the tender age of sixteen. We remained in the mist-filled van for about ten minutes, although it seemed forever. We were instructed not to remove our masks for at least fifteen minutes and to run around as the gas had penetrated our clothes. Most could not run around because the window in the mask had misted up. Mine hadn't – I had taken the pre-caution of rubbing half a potato across the window (good old Uncle George). It still works on car windows! The cardboard boxes that the masks came in soon disintegrated, my Mother and many others made a draw string bag to carry it, but it became a damned nuisance banging against our hips and was quietly often left at home.

Air raid shelters (Anderson)

Air raid shelters must have been a tremendous drain on the economy. They were useless, cold, damp and prone to flooding. Dad put three extra hutches in the shelter – the rabbits seemed to like it, after all, they were equipped for the cold and safer than us. The pelt trader who bought Mum's pelts commented on their quality.

Where did we sleep? My Mum and Dad decided to die in their bed, not in hospital with pneumonia. Jean slept in the back room, it was the safest. Where did I sleep? In the cupboard under the stairs with the brooms and the metres. I spent a good half hour organising a 'comfortable' nest for the night. The electricity metre was up on the wall whereas the gas metre was on the floor with about eighteen inches between it and the wall. I was not alone. I had Floss for company.

Air raid precautions

What a joke! That is until the muck hit the fan. It's surprising how quickly even the most stupid catch on. Us boys really came into our own. Just as we were able to identify motor bikes and cars simply by their engine noise, so it was with aircraft – ours, the Hun, make and model. We would tell the man on the telephone, he would inform a central plotter and the aircraft's every move would be followed.

Rationing

Rationing started slowly and steadily. My Mother ran up quite a debt with the Sopers 'club', she even enrolled my Dad, if he had known how much debt she had stuck him for! (Soper's was a departmental store in Harrow, where Debenham's was until 2018.)

Craftily she released the shirts, boots etc., as if she had pinched them from Churchill's wardrobe. My errand sock money and Post Office money all but a shilling went, the slogan was 'stock is better than money.' She was right as within a year there was nothing to buy and what there was, was rubbish.

My 1940's Boyhood

When? When? When?

'My brother Stan says it will be all over by Easter, Whitson at the latest.'

'In that case, why did he have that state of the art air raid shelter built in his garden? The one below ground level. It floods whenever we have a cup full of rain. Handy if an incendiary bomb should fall close by.'

My Father was about to say his two pennies' worth, but my Mother was in full flow.

'Also, Mr Lamont has rolled up the turf on his beautiful lawns, back and front and is wondering what to do with them, because everyone is doing the same thing – growing vegetables in case we have a long war. They nearly starved us out last time.'

'May I leave the table please, Mum?'

'Go on then, don't be late.'

I ran up the garden scattering chickens hither and thither.

I leaned on Mr Lamont's fence, 'Mum tells me that you are going to grow vegetables Mr Lamont.'

'Aye ladie that I am.'

'How are you going to manage for fertilizer? A handful here, a handful there, you will have spuds the size of marbles.'

'What's it to you ladie?' he said, giving me a shrewd look.

'Well, if you look behind our chicken coop, there is, what my parents call a compost heap. I call it a pile of poo, chicken and rabbit poo, all mixed up with pee soaked straw and sawdust.'

'How much?'

'Nothing. You supply us with vegetables from time to time and we supply you with compost, oh and would you like us to take your turf off you? There isn't a blade of grass left in our back garden. Chickens love grass.'

He filled his pipe and lit it.

'I will have to be having words with your parents. Can you ask them to come up the noo and have a chat.'

Once more I alarmed the chickens, then into the kitchen to brief Mum and Dad, their indifference shook me.

I really lost it! The prospect of an emerald lawn instead of the existing mudflat finally won her over. Once I had her on side, he was a push over. Many years later they told me that they had never seen me so angry.

I did try to help with the turf, but it were too much for me, besides 'I was more of a nuisance than a help,' Dad said. I could take a hint and went round to my best friend John's house. John's parents were very strict. He wasn't allowed out until he'd finished his homework, by then his friends were over the park. I didn't mind, their front room was a library, heaven for a 'book worm' like me. Sometimes they would let me take one or two books home carefully wrapped.

1940 was a very eventful year – Dunkirk, the Blitz. Northolt got off lightly compared to other towns and cities. We had a grandstand view of London burning from my parents' bedroom window, with St Mary's Church in Northolt, silhouetted against what looked like a glorious sunset.

However, the second stick of bombs landed in Mandeville Road shaking up the works of the Memorial Clock (the four sides told different times – none of them right for the rest of the war). More seriously, the roof of the Plough was burned off, fortunately the beer was in the cellar. We had some broken widows and our front door split and it was then that my Mother decided it was time that Jean and I were sent to live with her sister in the Swansea Valley.

Imagine taking a three year old and an eight year old to Paddington Station and putting them in a 'ladies only' compartment, filled with total strangers, then to be met by people who scarcely knew them at the other end.

For us, it was an adventure. What it did to my Mother, I never asked, I don't believe in opening old wounds.

No way in the world was I going to ride in a compartment filled with women! I would rather be in our hen coop. As soon as the train pulled out of the station I slipped into the packed corridor where I could be seen and settled on a kitbag listening to service men's talk. This was more my style.

When we arrived at Swansea Station, Jean was no longer singing and dancing but fast asleep across two laps. I had to give up my comfortable kitbag. Jean who still asleep, was slung across a porter's shoulder while I, holding his free hand, blundered along beside him.

'What do they look like? Boy bach?'

'I don't know.' Fortuitously my uncle and aunt put two and two together and spotted us.

We must have gone to Swansea Valley (Ysetalyfera) translated it means, and I kid you not, 'You catch the sheep.' Because that first week was a blur of Welsh and heavily accented English, my cousin's friends advised me tell the school that I was a year older, that way I would get into senior school. Big mistake! The standards were higher in Wales so I had to lift my game somewhat. The Beltons, that is my cousin Bill and my aunt and uncle, gave me a crash course in Welsh. The challenge was to be able speak to Bill's Great Grandmother, who spoke only Welsh. She was nearly a hundred years old, an incredible age at that time. Anyone who came from London or thereabouts was a bloody cockney. I was a novelty until some real East Enders arrived from West 'am, filling the Wern school to bursting point. Jean and I were spared the trauma of the 'cattle market', when the most attractive children were chosen first and siblings were split up, as happened to Brenda (my wife to be) and her brother, also many others. The locals had to take in evacuees regardless, they couldn't be blamed for refusing the poor and the ragged.

For me the most difficult part of fitting in was the walk or rather the climb up to the school, imagine walking twice the length of Roxeth Hill. First up, then down for lunch, up again after lunch and down again at teatime, no wonder my legs felt like rubber. One good side effect was to make them akin to tree trunks. Materially Jean and I were much better off. Uncle Tommy was a good provider. To give you an example, the Beltons had a top of the range push button HMV wireless. Uncle Tommy would listen to the traitor, late at night, nicknamed Lord Haw Haw. Having told Bill a story and got him off to sleep, I would slither to the top of the stairs and listen.

I can hear him now.

'Germany calling Germany calling. This is Germany calling on the 49 meter band, here is the news in English.'

I looked forward to the weekends when I went to stay with Gy Waen (Gy is Granny and Waen is moor land in Welsh).

My Grandmother's house was the last in a very long road looking out onto a vast moor. It had all the services apart from electricity, the builder went broke during the depression, consequently, the house was lit by oil lamps – a small one to light you to bed. I slept on the sofa in the huge kitchen, snug and warm with the light from the range to keep me company. My first task in the morning was to liven up the range, then collect a newspaper and a can of milk from the 'shop'. It really wasn't a shop, just one of the front rooms of a house, it never closed, if the front door was closed you simply went round the back.

The small oil lamps were only just adequate for their purpose, finding your way. Even the big reading lamp in the kitchen left a lot to be desired, so when my Grandmother (MnGy) popped out to visit a neighbour, I set to work and cut a zig-zag in the wick.

Magic! There was enough lamp light to read by. I waited until she said, 'light the lamp as you will ruin your eyes reading in this light.'

When my Grandfather commented on the improved light MnGy said, 'Raymond cleaned the wick.'

He examined the lamp then winked at me, 'Did he indeed,' then settled back with his newspaper.

I was reluctant to include this part of the story, but it happened, so here goes.

Not long after we arrived at the Belton's we were having breakfast when Jean said, 'Uncle Tommy, will you tell those nasty men not to sit on my bed and argue, they keep me awake.'

Fast forward many years, I happened to raise the matter with Uncle Tommy and my Auntie. They had, by then, moved from the Mansion into a three bedroom house. The Mansion belonged to Mr Bud, a Quaker iron master, who had a falling out with his partner during which the partner murdered Mr Bud. The family no longer wished to live in the mansion. Consequently, it was divided into five separate houses, in one of which the Beltons lived.

Bill and I were constantly on the lookout for Mr Bud, I even wrote a verse – *'Friday night is my delight, Mr Bud is on his flight. Whoooo!'* (Little sod!)

Over the years I have lived in three allegedly haunted houses. The first – Greenford. My Father maintained that as he settled the horses for the night, someone walked behind him and the yard dogs walked ahead of him cringing with their tails between their legs. When my Father came in the dogs scratched at the back door to be let in.

The second – Mr Bud.

The third – 187 Stoke Newington High Street, another Mansion, built in 1712 and owned by John Wilmer who suffered from Catalepsy. He arranged for a tomb to be built in his back garden with a string attached to his wrist, which would then be threaded through the wall and attached to a bell. If he was buried and should he stir, the bell would ring! Somebody cut the string!!

When Brenda and I lived there, it was a halfway house where we had one room, huge and difficult to heat, however, my dear Old Mum lugged an Aladdin paraffin stove across London, problem solved.

The nearest I got to seeing a ghost was one night during the black out. My friend, Robin Saunders, was the standby organist for St Mary's Church. When he went to practise on the organ and *boy* did he practice – Swing ... Jazz ... he played, I pumped.

I couldn't play the organ, however, on the linoleum I was a virtuoso. On the way out one evening we noticed a faint light over in the far corner of the graveyard. As we drew closer we realised that a man was digging a grave by the light of a candle, stuck in a niche in the side of the grave.

We asked the usual questions.

'Wasn't he scared working in a graveyard?'

'Nah, these wont 'urt yer,' he said waving a hand, 'it's the live buggers yer have to watch out for. I think this'll do, there's another one below.'

'How do you know?'

'Listen.'

He brought his spade down hard and there was a thud and a splintering sound.

'Coffin lid.' he said. 'Put me tools in the vestry and give us a hand.'

Many years later I met him again, he was a customer of mine. I was repairing his television – I would know that voice anywhere. He did remember the two boys in the church yard.

'Them was the days, eh Dolly.'

'Not 'alf. Most weeks over a 'undred cash in 'and.'

'Honest?'

'Oh yer.'

'I know you will think me rude, but why didn't you finish the war with a street of houses and a bungalow in Bournemouth?'

'Dogs 'n 'orses love, dogs 'n 'orses!' called his wife from the kitchen.

The Cinema

Now where were we? Oh yes, at my Welsh grandparents' house on the Waen [heath]. Like many veterans of war my Grandfather didn't talk about the war except to say he was with the Canadians at Vimy Ridge. He had been directed to do war work of some kind in Chepstow and only came home for a weekend once a month.

I got on well with them both. He was not a speak when you are spoken to type of granddad – so common in those days. This war, of course, not the 14/18 War, he would steer the conversation onto a different topic. If he didn't know the answer to one of my endless stream of questions, he would take out a note book and write my question in it and say, 'I don't know but I will find out.'

One weekend he brought home a Pears Encyclopaedia gift for me.

'Corn in Egypt,' my Grandmother exclaimed. I never did find out what she meant. I often think of that Encyclopaedia whenever the whipper snappers produce their 'tablets' to settle an argument.

Saturday's high spot was wheedling a few ounces of boiled sweets from shop keepers, then we would go to the cinema. The film had to be a good 'drama'. If it had Bette Davis in it so well and good, the downside, there is always a down side. Waiting for busses and then the long walk home. I didn't mind the walk home, it was the waiting. I have never been one for hanging about. I made inquiries about the footpath which connected the village with the two cinemas and debouched almost opposite my Grandparents' house. I told my Grandmother that I was going for a walk over the moor.

'Why?'

'I just fancy a stroll, it's a nice day.'

Off I went. The going was much better than I anticipated, six inches of coal waste, no mud. The path was used by miners from the village of the two cinemas as a short cut to the mine which was a few hundred yards from the foot path which explained the coal waste. If twenty miners brought a sack of waste every time they went home problem solved.

The foot path was about as long as we would have to walk from the bus stop to the house. All I had to do now was get the 'management' on side.

My Grandmother's walk-in larder was just that. The floor and shelves were blue slate cold in the summer and freezing in the winter. I went to her 'it might come in handy shelf.' There they were, many two pound empty jam jars with metal lids.

I scrounged a candle and cut it in half, melted some wax in the bottom of the jar and set the candle in the wax. Then poured about an inch of coal dust around it for support. Using a tin opener I perforated the tin lid, the candle had to breath, string wrapped around the neck of the jar made the hot jar easy to carry. One unforeseen benefit was it kept my hand warm. I did all this work in my Grandfather's shed. MnGy, easy going as she was, would take a dim view of me working on the kitchen table. My next task was to find out what its range was, no point in having it go out and plunge us into pitch darkness halfway along the path. Having told MnGy that I was going for a walk over the moor I set off.

About half way across I noticed that every now and again there would be a popping noise and the wick flared. Then it dawned, the coal dust was being 'cooked' giving off fire damp gas – the cause of many fires and explosions in coal mines, in future I used sand.

I couldn't wait for the film to end. At the bus stop I scrounged a light as in my haste I forgot to bring some matches. There was great interest in my contraption when I pulled it out of the leather bag and lit it, I had to put up with a lot of 'leg pulling.'

'If old Hitler sees that light he will bomb you.'

'He has been bombed twice already.'

'Third time lucky.' Typical Welsh dark humour.

The man who gave me the light walked at least a quarter of a mile with us, then, as he took leave of us he gave me a box of matches, 'Just in case.'

We walked in silence, no doubt MnGy wishing that she was waiting in the bus queue, then resigned to her fate she began discussing the film. That's more like it! Better still we didn't have to fumble around for a candle and matches to light the oil lamp when we got home.

Next morning I examined the jam jar lamp, there was still enough candle to do the walk again, the inside of the jar was a bit smoky, I cleaned the glass, replaced the candle, and we were ready for our next adventure.

My Grandmother was a very social person who loved concerts, plays and musicals, mostly Gilbert and Sullivan performed by the local operatic society. I enjoyed the music, what can I say about the actors capering about. Now that we had light to see us home we could go to the evening performances as well as the matinee, by the time I went back to the Belton's on Sunday evening I was exhausted.

I particularly liked the Granddad weekends as I called them, the grown up conversations. Granddad Joe Jones was very much into politics. His brother had started work at the age of twelve, his father having been killed in a mine accident. His wages having to help support a family of six, he became involved with the miners' union and went on to spend two years at Ruskin College Oxford, studying political and economic science and, after returning to South Wales, acted as a 'missionary' for the college and succeeded in persuading the South Wales Miners' Federation to establish ten scholarships to enable working miners to follow college courses. He was elected to Parliament in 1922 and resigned in 1931 when his wife used his rail pass without his knowledge. Of course, a modern MP with his hand in the till wouldn't do such a thing, such as fiddle his expenses. She had inadvertently done him a favour.

He began to travel, the Middle East, India, he was elected A.R.E.con.S. and published several books, two of which were *The Roots of British Power* (1949) and *India as a Future World Power* (1952). He died in 1970 and one of my few regrets is that I never met him. I had heard talk of him, mainly about the 'scandal.' If only I had known that he lived in Essex, so near to me. I was very busy in the '60's working my way through marriage, none the less, I would have visited him at least once, what a story he had to tell, ah well.

On the surface I was very happy with a large circle of friends, a kind uncle and aunt, but my cousin was a pain. When we went to bed he would start fighting and sooner or later Auntie would come up with the copper stick and I noticed that I got more than my fair share. I solved the problem by telling him stories.

He would soon drop off and I would creep to the top of the stairs and listen to Lord Haw Haw.

Home Again

I can't remember when or how it started, friends would say, 'What's the matter?' as my face crumpled, sometimes tears would flow, sometimes not, sympathy made it worse.

'I don't know,' I would mumble as I fled to the cloakroom or the empty playground. I was certainly not a wimp and could hold my own often against odds. In those days boys never cried, ever. Inevitably it happened at home, Bill spilled the beans, an interview with our doctor followed. I can still see his piercing blue eyes peering at me over his half specs. What was said I have no idea, after what seemed an age he dismissed me and told me to send in my aunt and uncle. They were in there for quite some time, I could hear them talking but not what they were saying. We walked home in silence, then my aunt said almost casually, 'Would you like to go home?' That did it.

I spent the next weekend with MnGy filled with guilt, and most of all, I felt I had betrayed her as she said, 'Poor love you couldn't help it. Write every month and tell me what you are doing.' I did.

The following Saturday I stood once again on the platform of Swansea station. Having watched London burn through my parents' bedroom window a few weeks later I watched Swansea burn. Not only the town but the Skewen oil refinery also, it took two weeks to put it out, and the stench hung around for months.

I settled down on a kit bag in the corridor trying to read but thinking about the chaos I caused, then I put myself in their shoes. They had rid themselves of an intractable problem. A broken leg is soon mended, but home sickness? I began to read my book and chat to the servicemen, as one remarked, 'I wish my bloody Commanding Officer would send me 'ome. I'm dead 'ome sick I am.'

I thanked a soldier for the use of his kit bag and lugged my case nearer the door. It was a better case than the one I took to Wales and fuller.

I waited for the train to slow before letting the window down, peering through the smoke and filth to see if I could catch a glimpse of her.

When people talk about pollution today, they haven't got a clue. I keep silent, what's the point?

Yes, there she is! She waves, I wave back. I'm home. I open the door, a hand firmly grasps my arm.

'In a minute Sonny, in a minute,' when the train lurched to a halt he released me.

'Thank you, sir!'

And I'm gone.

When my Mother took out a damp flannel from her handbag and wiped my grubby face, then hugged me, I knew that I WAS HOME.

It is strange how things turn out. I had expected a rebuke from my Mum for causing so much trouble. On the contrary, I had arrived home in the nick of time. She had been directed to manage the canteen of the Royal Army Ordnance Corps five days a week, also she managed to keep the job of 'posh cook' at the Target Pub in Northolt at weekends, cash in hand naturally. Cooks of her calibre were hard to find in peace time let alone war, when men and women not in the forces were 'directed' to work of national importance, catering to the wealthy was not under that category. However, there was a snag, there always is, juggling two jobs was hard enough.

'Chickens and rabbits?' I said.

'Yes, I am thinking of selling them, coop and all. It's a pity because I have lots of scraps for them.'

'You don't lug the scraps all the way from the Aladdin factory, do you?'

'Oh no. The Army have taken over the Racecourse (there used to be a horse racing course in Northolt which is now a housing estate) and the factories behind the Aladdin (this was the Aladdin paraffin heater factory). There is always a lorry going past our house and a burly squady jumps out of the lorry and puts the scraps in the trough.'

'The cost?'

'A bag of homemade cakes or a fruit cake.'

'Where do you get the fruit from?'

'None of your business.'

I was quite touched by the welcome that I got from Floss and Buster. They bounced around nearly knocking me over. I decide to take them over to the park while Mum was making dinner. They needed to let off some steam and when I took the bag of tatty old tennis balls and a racket out of the shed they went absolutely loopy.

Any misgivings I had harboured were smothered by the sound of those happy dogs as they chased the tennis balls. As I swung the racket I began to plan, it was quite obvious that Mr Hitler had done the women of Britain a favour. He had freed them from drudgery and most importantly given them a small brown envelope every Friday, their money. In the few months that I had been away the house had had an up lift, not quite to the Belton's standard. We still had the old PYE battery wireless. It had two batteries, a dry 120 volts and a lead acid 2 volt battery which needed recharging at least once a week at a cost of sixpence, a nice little earner for Mr Stevens our local electrician/wireless mechanic.

I didn't mind taking it and collecting it, what I couldn't stand was the queuing while he faffed about booking the batteries in and out.

One wet afternoon, I could stand it no longer.

'Mr Stevens, don't you think you could be more profitably employed mending a wireless or installing a power point instead of booking batteries in and out.'

He gave me a 'Cheeky little sod!' look.

'Somebody's got to do it.'

'I could do it in less than half the time. I'm willing to do a Saturday – your busiest day.'

'Give him a trial Love. I will keep an eye on him – what have you got to lose?'

He grudgingly agreed a second time as previously I was sent to Wales, unfortunately, three bombs and an exchange of telegrams had put the kybosh on that. The Saturday I was going to start my career as a booker in and out of batteries, but as you know that was the day my Mum sent my sister and me on a train to a foreign country where they spoke a foreign language and played a foreign game, Rugby. I did play – once I even held the ball for a micro second, until I was relieved of the burden by a sheep farmer's son. I heard the squelching boots of the games master's boots.

'How kind,' I thought, 'he's going to give me a hand up.' No such luck.

'Get up 'ooster – you are not bloody dead man!!'

'I'm not dead Sir, but I am dying.'

'No you're not, you're faking it.'

Then he put his boot into my ribs. At that moment rugby lost its charm for me.

When I duly took the battery to be charged I casually remarked that my offer still stood, Mr Stevens peered at me through a haze of smoke, he was a chain smoker.

'What offer?'

'You know, checking the batteries in and out.' The penny dropped.

'That cheeky little sod is back Love. Wants us to give him a trial.'

His wife came out from the back of the garage/workshop, 'Why not? Just for his cheek.'

'I am not cheeky Mrs Stevens, my Uncle Stan said that I was Bolshie and my Dad said I get it from my Mum.'

That's how I began to earn real money, instead of 'running errands money.' I became an electrician's mate crawling under floorboards dragging cable after me. Mrs Stevens supplied two pairs of overalls – one on, one in the wash. She had a large washing machine, the envy of her friends and neighbours.

Mrs Stevens often gave me an extra ten shillings or even a pound because I saved her from travelling in her husband's Reliant three wheeler death trap collecting bulky radiograms and stuff like cable and tools.

'Not a word to that mean old devil.'

I knew who she had in mind. They were not the happiest of couples, as she said, 'He loves the dog but tolerates me.' On the whole he was good to me – he even gave me driving lessons down on the industrial estate, on the q't, of course.

The Cronk

John was not evacuated, it would have interrupted his studies, in fact, he was working harder than ever. Oxford or Cambridge were in his sights, or rather his parents' sights.

John and I spent many happy hours in his Father's shed assembling an old cronk of a bike. I had warned John not to ride his Scholarship bike as I called it or someone, will as sure as eggs is eggs, pinch it.

'Why not keep your bike in my shed. Buster will look after it and ride this one when it's complete.'

'He has got a point John,' his Dad said. 'Every time you go out I wonder if we will ever see the bike again. Put it in Ray's shed and give Buster a bone every week.'

The cronk as we called it, consisted entirely of second hand parts salvaged from wrecked bikes. The local bike shop banked with John's Dad's bank. I had a vision of him standing on the platform of the bus in his pin stripe suit, bowler hat, brief case in one hand with a bicycle frame slung over his shoulder, stepping off and on the bus, doffing his hat to the ladies with aplomb. He was used to being stared at, he had a large dimple in his right cheek where a German bullet had entered his mouth and exited via his cheek.

'How are we going to make the Cronk unstealable?'

I suggested we paint it red, white and blue.

'How about red front rim and forks, blue mud guards, white frame and a black crank.'

John jumped at the idea.

'I was only pulling your leg John.'

'Well let's see what Mum and Dad think, okay?'

He was gone for quite a while.

I was keen to see the 'cronk' in all its glory the next time I visited.

'I must say you have done a beautiful job John, I was taken aback when I first saw it, to tell you the truth it's more me than you.'

'Mum will be pleased. It was she who painted it, she said she wouldn't trust Dad and me with a hairbrush never mind a paint brush.'

'You can come out now Mum, he likes it.'

'Aren't you going for a ride on your new bike, Raymond?'

I will draw a veil over what happened next.

John had the use of the cronk until we built another cronk. On Saturday I took a plump oven ready chicken and a tin of Balkan Subrani pipe tobacco, gold dust, being a coal merchant had its advantages. That tobacco must have cost all of a hundred weight of coal.

'Tell him it's from me,' my Dad said.

In less than a month there were two Technicolor bikes on the street, and John's scholarship bike was guarded by Buster.

In the olden days, 'teenagers,' the word hadn't been invented then, but we were teenagers just the same. We were not allowed to mope around the place complaining that we were bored and had nothing to do. Consequently I placed an ad in a newsagent's window, advertising my services as a gardener. My Mother was most unkind and said, 'she would pay me to stay out of her garden!'

However, a very upper middle class lady, Samantha (she had a double barrelled surname which I have forgotten), contacted me. Her day job was personal private secretary to Sir something or other, who was a big cheese at EMI. She gave me quite a grilling. She had expected someone older, however, I would be cheaper. I think that my being a boy scout and in the choir of St Mary's helped. You had to be a chorister if you wanted to be a scout. She knew nothing about gardening, she just wanted it kept tidy, which was fine with me.

I borrowed a sickle and a sharpening stone from Mr Bishop, one of our neighbours, who showed me how to use and sharpen it, a very kindly old man. I resolved to buy him an ounce of tobacco with my first week's pay.

As my Mother would say 'it never rains but it pours.' I had no sooner settled into my gardening job, than Sam, as I was told to call her, asked me whether I knew of someone who was a first class ironer. She had a standard to maintain in the office and was rather surprised when I turned up one evening with Brenda. After a lot of argument, she produced a badly creased white blouse.

'See what you can do with this.'

Without a word Brenda began work.

'I cannot stand idly by and watch a perfectly good blouse ruined, I am going to put the kettle on.'

Over tea and biscuits Brenda and Sam talked money.

'Blouses four pence each, anything with pleats, sixpence.'

'That's not what I had in mind Brenda.'

'I know exactly what you had in mind Samantha.' Brenda looked her in the eye. 'I don't need the money, I am here to please Ray.'

'I told you Darling what her reaction would be, didn't I?' I nodded. 'Come along Ray.'

'Thank you for the tea and biscuits, Samantha.'

'Just a moment you two. Four pence and six pence. Okay?' She held out her hand.

As I walked her to the bus stop I congratulated her on looking a million dollars. 'Do you really think so?'

'I took a leaf out of your Mum's book – be poor, look poor and the rich will do it on you. The shoes, stockings, dress, coat, hat and gloves belong to a very good friend, they are rather posh. She also loaned me this pretty watch, it doesn't work, who will notice? I will get it repaired by way of a thank you. What do you think?'

'Brilliant, better than a box of chocolates, that is assuming you can find a box.'

I also congratulated myself on my good fortune, a casual meeting over the park. She and her brother were there on their bikes, some yobs had stolen the contents of her saddle-bag and were trying to wrestle her bike off her. I walked up to the one pinching the bike and without a word gave him straight fingers to the solar plexus, he collapsed in a heap.

'Next!' I said to the other three with my heart in my mouth.

Quickly gathering up the contents of her saddle bag I ordered, 'Follow me!'

Her poor brother was ashen as well he might be, he wouldn't have stood a chance against that four. Nor would I. Luckily they were on foot.

I escorted her home to Ruislip Close, chatting all the way, her brother bringing up the rear. She impressed me no end, what she thought of me I never asked. I must have made a favourable impression though, because she accepted an invitation to the cinema on Saturday. And that is how the tribe began.

She was very attractive with her 'Greek' hairdo, the Hungarian blouse and the dirndl skirt.

At That Moment It Happened

This is one of the many compositions I wrote, to overcome the tedium of being shut in a concrete cylinder with forty-five or more bored children. The teachers, once we were sat down, would put on their helmets and go outside to watch 'the fun' leaving us to our own devices.

Mr Davis would leave us with, 'Read them one of your Penny dreadfuls, Wooster.'

The raids usually lasted about half an hour, the siren being triggered by enemy air craft passing over on their way to their target. To hear their chatter you would think they wanted to be bombed. Several bombs had fallen on Northolt but nothing like the pasting other towns had.

The more scary and suspenseful the story, the better they liked it.

The only sound was the scratching of steel nibs on paper, no whispering or talking in Mr Davis's class.

Then it happened – the toe curling, stomach churning sound of an air raid siren.

'Stand, put your work away, chairs on your desks.'

'Lead on Chambers.'

He was the class monitor, nice bloke, not jumped up as so many monitors were, altho' I did hate him for his exquisite handwriting.

The class of forty-five filed out silently, no pushing or shoving or messing about, this was serious business. Mr Davis pushing Brenda Wallace in her cumbersome wheelchair, Brenda holding the register in one hand and the gavel in the other brought up the rear. We also had another polio victim in our class, Nobby Clark. He had half an iron from his right foot to his knee but none the less he was pretty nimble, both Nobby and Brenda made light of their infirmities.

'Emergency escape hatches secured and vents open,' Chambers shouted from the other end of the concrete tube that we called an air raid shelter. I ran back to the school where Mr Davis was having difficulty getting Brenda and the wheelchair down the steps.

'Let me give you a hand, Sir.' I took the front wheels. Success! 'Thank you, Wooster. I thought for a moment I was going to tip you out Brenda.'

At that moment it happened, the unmistakable sound of a Junker 88's twin engines.

'Run Sir, run! It's a Junker and it's very close!'

I put my weight behind the chair, took the register and gavel and threw them into the shelter.

Grabbing an arm each, Sir and I bundled poor Brenda through the doorway, whilst Sir clanged the steel blast proof door shut. Wilkins helped me to dump Brenda on the bench seat as she bent forward to release her knee straps. At that moment it happened – the unmistakable shriek and whistling sound of a falling bomb. I grabbed her legs and dragged her down onto the duck boards and protected her as best I could.

The exploding bomb – a near miss – shook the shelter as a terrier would a rat decanting the children off the benches into a writhing screaming tangle of arms and legs.

At that moment it happened, the lights flickered on and off, twice, then went off, good old reliable Chambers had remembered to light the two oil lamps, one at each end of the shelter. Through the bedlam and chaos a voice rang out.

'Silence!! ... WILL YOU BE QUIET! ... I am going to call the register. Adams are you injured?'

'No Sir.'

'Atkins are you injured?'

'No Sir.'

And so on through the forty-five.

'It would seem, that apart from some heads being knocked together and we do need some heads knocking together don't we, Eves and Smith?'

'Yes Sir.'

'Everyone is fine.'

'It would appear that our shelter has protected us.'

'Three cheers for the builders.'

Mr Davis made his way to the other end of the shelter, climbed the ladder and held a muffled conversation with Chambers.

Standing at the foot of the ladder Sir made the following announcement. 'It would seem children, that the bomb has dumped a large quantity of dirt on our shelter and the one next door. The heavy rescue teams are hard at work trying to clear it, meanwhile, lots of goodies will be passed down to us, things that we have not seen for a long time, through the vent.'

'Sir, Sir, There is water on the floor, it's coming in through cracks in the wall.'

'Come down Chambers, I want to speak to the Rescue Team.'

What he said I don't know, but by the time, the anti-blast door opened and the water gushed out, the water was up to our knees even tho' we were standing on the benches.

Two hefty boys stood on either side of Brenda propping her up, she must have been in agony, with the metal leg irons cutting into her thighs.

'Won't be long now Brenda, don't worry,' Sir reassured her. Brenda gave him one of her smiles.

'I'm fine Sir, with Adams on one side of me, Buckland on the other, and you to catch me if I fall, what could go wrong?'

A few weeks later we were back to normal scratching paper with our nibs, when it happened. I heard a strange noise. I looked round others had heard it to. Mr Davis was crying.

What to do? We carried on with our work.

Chambers, the ever reliable Chambers, left the room quietly and came back with the Headmaster who took Mr Davis away, never to be seen or spoken of again.

Mr Davis's breakdown did happen, the rest of the story was one of my compositions I made up to entertain my fellow 'prisoners'.

The Allotments

When my junior school resumed in September, the boys' first task was to dig up the produce that the previous boys had planted earlier in the year at their parents' expense. Potatoes and carrots were put into Hessian sacks, the onions were plaited into strings ready for the teachers to take home.

The year that I was due to move from junior school to senior school, I laid plans. We boys knew that the teachers were, as one boy said, 'coming it'. But in the best English tradition this year was going to be different. I began by collecting Hessian sacks, reorganising the shed and strengthening my trolley. I had better explain about the trolley. It consisted of a plank of wood. This was the chassis. Two pairs of wheels were usually from an old pram, the front one steerable by a length of string, rather like reins. A wooden box sat on the chassis, handy for carrying things or sitting in.

When mid-August came, I modified the fence so that it would admit me and my trolley. So I began work, waiting, of course, until the Caretaker had gone home. A few evenings saw my plot cleared. As I gazed around the other plots, I thought about the aching void in the shed. Over tea, I asked my Mother casually, if she would pay half a crown for the contents of each of the other plots. Bobby Buckland, Arthur Connor, et al, trooped round to have their palms greased with silver. It was then that I realised I had bitten off more than I could chew, never mind, rain or shine, the plots would be cleared.

Unfortunately, I became careless and went there during working hours and sure enough, the Caretaker came ambling down one afternoon.

'What are you a' doin' of?'

I explained why I was there.

'You've no business a-bein' here. Give us yer name. Now clear off and don't let me see you round here again.'

Taking my spade, fork and trolley, I made my way out through the main gate. He hadn't spotted the modified fence. From then on it was all evening work.

In September, I duly changed schools. The first day we had the usual boring, boring assembly. At the end of assembly we were ready to return to our classes.

'Raymond Wooster, come to the front.' Which I did.

'Wait outside my office.'

I could feel hundreds of eyes on me. Like me, their minds were filled with fear and awe. I was escorted to the head's office and left outside to wonder, I hadn't been at the school long enough to have committed any undiscovered crime!

The headmaster opened his office door, 'Inside! Stand there!'

I stood in front of the desk. The head sat opposite me in his chair; reached out and took an ash stick from his umbrella stand. He held the stick in both hands, flexing it in a meaningful way. This was not the Malacca cane which was known as a 'stinger' by us boys. It was a 'finger breaker' about half an inch thick.

'So we have a thief in our midst, do we?'

'I don't understand, Sir.'

'Well you soon will!'

He brought the stick down with a resounding thwack on the desk.

'I have been informed that you have stolen produce from the allotment at your previous school, did you not?'

'No Sir. My parents paid for it and I grew it. It's theirs by right.'

Thwack!

'By right? How dare you talk to me about right. This is a police matter. Which means Borstal. I would rather have you in Borstal than in my school. However, if you are prepared to take my punishment, we will say no more about it. What do you say?'

'I think you should discuss this with my parents first, Sir. As my Mother says, "Right is right and wrong is no man's right".'

Thwack! He leaned across the desk.

'Are your parents Bolsheviks?'

'I don't know, Sir.'

'Don't know? Don't know?'

'What is a Bolshevik, Sir?'

I noticed that when I mentioned my parents coming up to the school, his attitude changed. I knew my Father, being English, would not come up to the school, but, my Mother, being a Welsh Tigress would defend her cub providing that is, he was in the right, to the death.

The headmaster picked up a book from his desk and asked, 'Do you know what this is, Wooster?'

'It is a Bible, Sir.'

'Right Wooster. I want you to take this Bible in your right hand and promise me that you will never remove anything from the junior school allotments.'

I gave my word with a glad heart for there was nothing more to be had.

The Explosives

During the war, the Northolt Racecourse was a paradise for us village boys, scrambling nets and knotted ropes hung from the branches of tall elms, oaks and gantries.

Before the war the Gaumont British film studios, where they filmed outdoor scenes was just off Islip Manor Road, were our playground after the staff had gone home. The so-called security staff were aged and couldn't catch a cold. Sabu the star of the film *Jungle Book* stayed in the Manor House while he was filming. In the evenings he would drive his petrol-engined boy sized racing car round the extensive grounds – we peasants would gaze through the wire fence in the forlorn hope that he would invite us in, he never did.

Where was I? Oh yes, the army training ground. We always waited until four o'clock, that's when they marched off to tea. We learned the hard way that fit soldiers were fleet of foot and we were no match for them.

A clip round the ear and 'Bugger off' was our reward.

Once they were gone the training ground was ours, the scrambling nets were favourite. We couldn't wait to be eighteen and called up – stupid boys! We didn't want to be Squaddies. We wanted to be pilots, fighter pilots for preference.

There was one piece of kit that intrigued us.

Watching from the 'safe' side of the fence we saw an area covered with single beds, these were covered with turves. When the sergeant blew his whistle the men in training would crawl under the bed steads while the corporals would throw thunder flashes, a kind of firework, which exploded with tremendous bang! The whole idea being to get them used to battle conditions – no wonder we all wanted to be pilots. When they were safely out of sight we would start scouring the training ground for thunder flashes that had not gone off for some reason or other.

We would take our loot to Arthur Connor's shed, no one would bother us there. Splitting the cardboard cylinder with a safety razor blade we extracted the silver coloured powder.

Having received a chemistry set for Christmas I knew all about these things, they thought. Then I made several fuses out of thin string and candle wax inserted one into a small pile of the silver powder, lit it and as they say, retired immediately. It did not go bang, more flash and a fizz; we assumed that the powder must have been wet.

I am not one to give up easily, so we harvested even more thunder flashes.

Now with a goodly heap of silver powder, we gave it another go. I duly lit the fuse which burned into the pile, it fizzed a bit and seemed to go out, for some reason I clapped my hands to my face.

Why I don't know, my Uncle George had told me, 'If you hear one coming Tosh, lay down, put your hands over your face clamp your nostrils and put your thumbs in your ears, and most important of all clench your buttocks. An exploded gut is a slow and pain full death.'

He should know. He went into the Navy aged fourteen from an orphanage and fought the Turks at Gallipoli aged sixteen. He remembers boys of sixteen being shot for cowardice, officers were sent home in disgrace. Uncle George was very bitter about that.

I didn't hit the deck but I did follow his other instructions, consequently I did not lose my sight, altho' the backs of my hands were badly burned. My handwriting went from bad to worse and I spent three weeks in King Edwards' Hospital being spoon fed by a harassed Yugoslav nurse who plied me with questions. As soon as I answered one she popped another spoonful of herring into my mouth, bones and all.

As if that was not punishment enough, I had to have three warm saline baths a day, that was how sophisticated burns treatment was in those days.

The worst part came in the following months, the slightest tap on the backs of my hands and large blood blisters would appear. I immersed my hands in a saline solution morning and night. I did not go out to play for fear of infection. These were the days before antibiotics. Already a voracious reader I almost lived in our local library.

When I came out of hospital I asked my Mother if she had seen my chemistry set anywhere?

Came the reply, 'It's where you left it.' Stupid boy – it was probably down the dump.

The Milk Thief

In the olden days, before breakfast clubs and free dinners and fruit, if a child paid his or her teacher 'tupence happeny' equivalent to a penny in new money, he or she received a third of a pint of milk at playtime. As the war progressed the third of a pint bottles were withdrawn and we had to take mugs into school. Our third was poured from a pint or two pint bottle. The teacher was unaware that we were watching like hawks and we noticed that she often took an unopened pint bottle home in her leather patchwork bag.

We ring leaders were given notes to be given to Mr Mole, our headmaster. From that day on the milk was doled out from a measure.

Looking back it seems a fuss about nothing, however with rationing so strictly enforced, our sense of fair play was razor sharp, we were always hungry but never starving, unlike the poor devils in Europe. We had our 'back yard farm' thanks to the kindness of Mr Green and Mr Croxtan. In return they got a roast chicken or rabbit and half a dozen eggs every now and then.

I hated killing a chicken or a rabbit, eviscerating them was even worse, my Mother instructed me. Being a country girl, it was all second nature to her. Her 'be kind, strike hard and fast,' did not come easy to a wimp like me. I had to be careful with the rabbits. If I punctured the gall bladder it would spoil the flesh. Fortunately, I didn't have to skin the rabbits – I wasn't strong enough. I escaped plucking the chickens – my finger and thumb became red raw. My worst nightmare was to have my friends come round the back and surprise me with my hand in a chicken's bottom pulling its entrails out. it was the very least that I could do for my overworked Mother. How the women coped is a mystery. However, they had the comfort of that brown envelope, their money.

At least we were making financial progress. Her 'good boy' was reward enough.

You will have gathered by now that this memoir and the incidents are not strictly in order, memories trigger other memories so, if you think that I am going to go to the trouble of sorting the muddle and mess of my life just to please a pedant like you – TOUGH!!!

Here is a typical instance of events out of sync.

The Coal Wharf

One of my favourite places was the Harrow Met Coal Wharf. since we moved into 28 Mandeville my Dad ran his, by now one horse, coal business from the Harrow Met wharf. If I didn't have the bus fare I would walk to South Harrow market, offer to sweep up the green grocer's stall or make myself useful in some other way. When I had finished, Mr Jones would give me a sixpence. I would doff my cap and thank him, then be on my way, but not before I had bought a Milky Way. I would have preferred a Mars Bar but my sixpence did not cover a Mars Bar and the bus fare to the wharf.

When I arrived at the wharf, I made my way to where the loaders were emptying several trucks and filling coal bags which they then loaded onto lorries. Taking out my pad and pencil, the men wrote their order on a separate sheet, cigarettes, hot meat pies, etc. They would sign the sheet which I would hand to the pie-shop man who would duplicate the order, put it in a paper bag which would go in my shoulder bag. The contents would be paid for when they went home. It sounds complicated but it worked, the loaders gave me a few coppers for my trouble.

One of the loaders, Uncle Maf, 'worked' for his brother, Uncle Stan. As a child, Maf had shown great promise, passed the eleven plus and was assured of an office job in the family business when he left school. Sadly, Maf had one flaw. He was bone idle. Uncle Maf lived with my grandmother and off his Brother Stan. It was the proud boast of the Woosters that they all die in harness – that was not going to be his fate.

When my grandmother died, Uncle Stan managed to get Maf into Shenley, the local psychiatric hospital. Nothing mad about Maf: when he was given a job, he protested.

'I have not come here to work, I have come here to be understood!' They eventually found him a job in a local pub!

You may wonder why I call him Maf. I pulled my Mother up, 'why don't you call him Mathew?'

'Because his name is Mafeking. He was born when Mafeking was relieved and his father decided to call his first born son, Mafeking, in honour of the event, poor devil, no wonder he took to drink.'

I was on my way to the gate one evening when Maf asked me to help him finish emptying a coal truck. 'Won't take long, about half an hour. Just chuck it on the ground. I'll give you sixpence.' It took a while longer than he said, but sixpence is sixpence.

I knew that I had been cheated when he began rummaging in his pockets. 'See me next Saturday, Raymond.'

I knew it was useless to argue. He wanted to get to the pub to spend my sixpence.

On the bus going home I hatched a plan. I would not appeal to Uncle Stan whose hand would fly to his pocket instantly, I didn't need the money, my 'running errands money' would see me through the week. The more I thought about it, the more I liked it. What was that phrase I had read somewhere? 'Revenge is a dish best eaten cold.'

Then it happened. I was summoned into the office. It wasn't an office, it was a large shed divided in two, one half for the loaders to dry off or cook. My Dad warned me not eat anything cooked in the frying pan, he showed me the rats' footprints in the congealed fat.

Where was I? 'Oh yes, in the office. Dad, Uncle Stan and Uncle Maf, who looked very angry. Uncle Maf tells us that you are very rude to him and you don't answer him when he speaks to you,' my Dad said.

'And if happens again, Harold I am going to box his bloody ears.'

'You will do no such thing Maf, there must be a very good reason for his behaviour.'

Uncle Stan put his arm around my shoulders, 'Well, Raymond?'

I told my story, my Dad said I looked as cool as a cucumber. I didn't feel cool, my heart was going like a steam hammer. As I expected Uncle Stan's hand flew to his pocket. 'No Uncle Stan, Uncle Maf owes me and he must pay.'

Maf reluctantly fumbled in his waistcoat pocket, drew out a sixpence and handed it to me mumbling.

'Why didn't you say?'

When we got home, Dad gave me a ten shilling note. 'From Uncle Stan. Be sure to thank him next time you see him.'

'Yes Dad.'

The Shunting Engine

The most enjoyable time for me in the coal yard was riding on the shunting engine.

While delivering the pies and tobacco to the loaders, I remarked to the foreman that I would like to ride in the cab of the engine and thought no more about it.

The following Saturday, the foreman said, 'Do you still want to ride in the shunting engine, Sonny?'

'Oh yes please, Sir.'

'Well in that case, come along a me.'

The engine was at the water tower taking on water, the fireman scrambled down. 'You want to be an engine driver, do you?'

Without waiting for an answer he picked me up and placed me on the foot plate as if I was a bag of feathers. 'Young feller is after your job, driver.'

The driver who was seated on the other side of the foot plate, turned and smiled, 'Does 'e now?'

I was intrigued by the way they addressed one another. They never used their names, always driver and fireman. Not for them pies from the café, they fried bacon and eggs on a hot shovel. I promised to bring my own bread, bacon and eggs next time.

I was in my seventh heaven as we shunted the trucks hither and thither, lurching and the music of the buffers as they crashed into one another. After a couple of hours, they had to go off to Pinner. Ah well. it was nice while it lasted.

The Blackout

When I was a child the streets were gas lit, after dark the lamps would create a pool of light around their base in which we children would play various games, or attach a rope to the cross bar and swing round until we crashed into the lamp post. Hours of fun, until we were called in at bedtime. The blackout as it was called put stop to all that. The slightest chink of light would cause a policeman to knock on your door with a warning or fine. More people were killed in motor accidents than in air raids in the first two years of the war.

On clear nights the stars shone in a black velvet sky, the moon or 'the bombers' moon' as it was called lit up everything. We boys knew every constellation especially if we were Boy Scouts. We Scouts were being trained to be messengers, rather like the ones in the siege of Mafeking during the Boer

War. Most of us were proficient in Morse and semaphore. The most enjoyable were wide games. Three boys would go off into the dark, when the Scout Master blew his whistle they then had to make their way back to the Scout hut and deliver a message without getting apprehended.

I, as they say, 'devised a cunning plan.'

A brook wended its way through Northolt passing within a hundred yards of the hut. I hid a pair of plimsolls in the long grass on the bank of the brook. When it was my turn to be one of the messengers, I quickly located my plimsolls, took off my shoes, stuffed my socks in my shoes, tied the laces together and draped them around my neck. I needed plimsolls, as there might be broken glass in the ankle deep water.

Slowly and carefully I made my way towards the bridge adjacent to the hut, the 'Germans' were busy talking, giving away their positions. I lobbed a lump of brick which fell with a thud on the grass. There was a chorus of 'What was that?' then I lobbed another half a brick.

'He's on the other side of the bridge, spread out everybody.'

One or two 'blue light torches' scanned the village green for a moment and then were turned off. Meanwhile, I dried my feet on the abundant grass, put on my socks and shoes, hid my plimsolls in the grass then crept into the churchyard and waited for the Scout Masters' 'it's over whistle.' I joined the others, keeping silent in the pitch dark, entered the Scout hut and handed my 'message' to the Scout Master without a word.

Our Scout Master demanded that I tell him how I managed to elude the 'Germans.'

'Sorry Father, I might have to do it for real some day.'

For a Vicar he was most unforgiving and arrogant. My Mother had a run in with him, I had been singing wedding solos on Saturdays, but the coal wharf and the shunting engine was a greater attraction, also the Vicar received thirty shillings per solo of which I got ten shillings. Originally, he got the lot, until I pointed out that I would rather go to

Saturday morning pictures than sing, to which he replied, 'Think of the honour.'

I patted my pocket. 'This is my honour, Father.'

'Ten shillings then?'

'Providing that I am finished by eleven, Father.'

I reasoned that if I finished by eleven I would have time to dash home, change into my work clothes, catch the 140 bus and be at the wharf by lunch time.

Eventually I gave up the singing, Scouts and also the wharf in favour of checking in batteries and doing simple electrical repairs for Mr Stevens. More importantly, I was in the warm and dry, except when I was delivering and collecting batteries on my colourful bike.

I modified a pram chassis. My Dad had a draw bar made. An orange box lined with straw made the batteries snug and safe. This collection and delivery service meant that Mr Stevens had to buy another charger, second-hand of course.

The customers paid me and gave me some coppers for my trouble – no trouble!

At last things were beginning to improve, my Post Office Savings book was plump and I could afford to buy Christmas and birthday presents, not that there was much to buy. It didn't take long to use up the clothing coupons in my Ration Book. By 1942 everyone was heartily sick of this 'bloody war' and its shortages. Little did they know, there was worse to come. Even bread was rationed. If they had known that rationing would not end until the early 50s, I don't know what would have happened.

The 'powers that be' kept drumming it into the peasants that we must feed starving Europe. If you had money or if you kept livestock in your back garden, things were not too bad.

Uncle Stan's pig

My Uncle Stan owned a yard next to Harrow Park. He bought it off his Uncle Sid for three shillings a week, yes three shillings a week!! That was during the thirties, I kid you not. He had several stables which became obsolete when he switched to motors.

One of the stables became a snug home for a 'weaner', that is a one month old baby pig. It cost Uncle Stan a hundred-weight of coal. The piglet was bound and gagged, popped into an empty coal sack. It may seem cruel to a pig lover, but a vocal wriggling pig in a coal sack would draw the attention of the Constabulary. The Constable maybe amenable to a 'drink' or the promise of a hock, some time in the future. On the other hand it could mean six months in Wormwood Scrubs as a guest of His Majesty The King. Get my drift?

The pig, fattened over several months, was ready for slaughter. One rainy Sunday morning, while my Mother was at work, my Dad and I set off on our bikes for Uncle Stan's yard. Uncle Stan's Jack, he was a butcher by trade. My Dad and I were to, as my Dad said, do the 'business.'

My job entailed manoeuvring the tin bath in order to catch the blood and guts, also to position the Hurricane lamps. I noticed that Uncle Stan's son Jimmy wasn't there. He was about three years older than me, and was a 'sensitive soul' as his Mother explained at one of the afternoon teas.

I have often seen my Mother angry. She had plenty to be angry about, but when she found out that I had helped to slaughter the pig her fury was unbridled. I got washed and changed and fled round to my friend John's house. They were very good, behaved quite normally. I am sure they sensed something in the air, I stayed for tea. Just as well I hadn't eaten since breakfast.

The storm lasted for more than a week on, and off. Fortunately, she did not throw the six pork chops at him.

Plane Spotting

The winter of 40/41 was particularly cold fortunately. My mother had purchased two pairs of 'combs' as they were known, one on and one in the wash. How times have changed. When I described them to my children and grandchildren they were horrified. 'Wouldn't be seen dead in them,' was the general verdict. It gets better. When I describe my lovely bunny-rabbit skin jacket with mittens to match – oh and I forgot my fur hat – they went loopy. Me? I loved it, snug as the proverbial bug.

My rig-out was perfect for plane spotting with the fire watchers. As well as doing a full day's work, men were required to do a couple of hours 'fire watching' just in case a careless German should drop a few incendiary bombs.

My task was to identify aircraft, ours or theirs. The grown ups couldn't tell the difference between a duck and a Dornier. It was the same when we were haymaking on Northolt airfield. I was the boy leading the horse, airfields were being shot up left right and centre. I was instructed that if I heard a Jerry plane I was to give the loaders a shout and run and jump in the ditch. 'What about the horse?'

'Don't you worry about that old 'orse, she'll either do nothin' or bolt.' What a thing to brag about in school on Monday. Stupid boy!!

My biggest enemy was boredom. Fortunately I always carried a couple of Penguin books inside my jacket. During our breaks I would read the *Daily Herald* and the *Daily Mirror* to the loaders, they had had very little schooling. One of the loaders was related to the Billy Smart Family Circus and had travelled the country far and wide.

The best part of the job was when we worked near the maintenance hangers listening to the ground crews telling us of the exploits of the 'Bloody mad Poles', our 3o3 amo' was 'nbg'[1] so when they ran out of amo' they wrecked Jerry's tail. Didn't do the Hurricane much good either, nice bit of flying tho'. What about the rear gunner? 'Oh they always kill him first so if you join the Air Force don't be a tail end Charlie.' Sound advice!

The Canadian Cousin

My Canadian cousin came to visit, he let me play with his gun! My poor mother was terrified.

'Don't worry any, Gwen, I've taken all the shells out.'

Boy did I brag at school the following day.

He survived Diepe, D DAY and the rest, went home where his tractor turned over and killed him.

The Yanks

When the Japanese kicked America's back door in, the Yanks decided to leave the touch line and join in the game. They had already helped us out with Lease Lend. We paid the last

[1] Nbg = no bloody good

arrival was fill the two large chaff sacks I had brought with ferns, hacked down with Mr Hutt's trusty knife.

As I worked I wished I could tell him what a treasure the knife had been over the years, but there. We were sleeping in 'permanently' erected bell tents, much better than ridge tents, each sleeping space had a ground sheet. I put my sack of ferns between the ground and the sheet. I didn't need two sacks of ferns so I gave one sack to Robin Saunders. He was pathetically grateful, within three days there wasn't a fern to be seen let alone had.

One other amenity, the swimming pool, about twenty feet by ten filled with pea green water, available for swimmers only, not less than three boys in the pool at any one time.

The Head Scout (the Vicar) explained that should one of the boys drown, the pool would have to be drained in order to recover the body, and then refilled. 'A frightfully expensive business.'

The phrase entered our vocabulary ending with, 'Donche now!'

He never once realised that we were 'extracting the urine'. I must have been our dead pan faces.

As they say all good things come to an end.

There was much talk in the tent that last night about how many of our soldier friends would survive the coming invasion. One of the sergeants gave an impromptu speech on the last night ending with, 'we are doing this for you, so don't mess it up'.

1945 - And all that

When the war with Germany ended everyone seemed to expect things to return to 'normal.' They didn't. Rationing

instalment in the early twenty-first century. I don't think the Russians paid a bean.

I was given strict instructions to be polite to the Yanks and not pester them for gum. As I passed my first Yank I doffed my cap as I would a neighbour and wished him, 'Good morning, Sir.'

A few paces further on I heard, 'Hey kid, come here.'

'Yes, Sir.'

'That was kinder polite kid.'

I explained.

'That's real nice of your parents, der yer lighk candy kid?'

'What's candy, Sir?'

He pulled a Hershy bar from his pocket. 'Oh a chocolate bar, Sir. I haven't seen a chocolate bar for a long time.'

'Here kid take it.'

'I couldn't possibly,' I explained what my parents had said about pestering Americans for sweets and gum.

'Take it,' he ordered.

'Thank you, Sir. I will send it to my little sister. She has been sent away to somewhere safe away from the bombing.'

He wasn't the last kind Yank whom I greeted.

V1 Doodle Bug. V2 Rocket

The V1 OR DOODLE BUG as we called it, sounded rather like that motorbike which roars along your street in the early hours of the morning. It brings out the worst in people, a different kind of worst, whereas you wish the bikie in hell.

When you heard a doodle bug, you murmured, 'Keep going, keep going.' Rather selfish I agree but there, once the engine stopped the V1 would plunge to earth creating a relatively small crater but a tremendous blast.

This is where Uncle George's advice came in handy. Hit the deck, protect your face and clench your buttocks. If only they had put those simple instructions on those stupid propaganda leaflets they put through our letter boxes, I wonder how many would have survived?

V2 – Not much to say about them, they didn't tell you that they were coming until after they had arrived. They travelled at supersonic speeds. Not cricket you must agree.

I much preferred the old fashioned iron bombs of which we received about half a dozen or so. The VIs, we were lucky, only three. The unsporting V2s, none that I am aware of.

Camping with the Scouts

The enjoyable thing about shortage, is that pleasures are more intense whenever they occur and are shared. It often amuses me whenever I hear people and their children complain.

'Oh no, not Disney World again!'

I suppose you can have too much of good thing. On the other hand, it was just as well the Health and Safety brigade did not do an assessment on our holidays. Transport for a start, an old rickety sand and ballast lorry filled with all our kit and caboodle, topped off with at least twenty-five Scouts. Fitting in or holding on as best they can, the Scout Master being a Vicar, had a ration of petrol. He and the three Senior Scouts travelled in his luxurious Morris Eight.

We didn't care, this was our adventure of the year. We would have travelled by dung cart, maybe not, but you get my drift.

Our first camp was at a place called Boars hill, just outside Oxford about thirty miles from London. It had been a large scouting venue for some years, unfortunately half the a[...] had been taken over by the army for training purpos[...] were not allowed to pass any trees ringed with blue pa[...] army trained with live ammunition, which cram[...] foraging for firewood. Fortunately they had an ope[...] tion to join us every evening around the campfi[...] singsong. They always arrived with cookhouse food[...] of wood, and regaled us with tales of daring do.

One morning we were walking into Oxford – So[...] march. When we passed a German prisoner of wa[...] knew that they were Germans because there was[...] POW camp in South Harrow and their uniforms[...] distinctive. One of the Scout Leaders ran to th[...] threw a packet of cigarettes over the wire. Ther[...] pede of prisoners towards the packet. The Br[...] immediately reversed their rifles and began [...] butts at the POWs. They didn't connect – fortu[...]

One of the guards picked up the cigarettes and[...] Troop Leader over. As he handed over the [...] didn't mince his words. 'Never give these Ba[...] they are the scum of the earth. All of 'em wa[...]

The Leader was about to protest.

'An anuver fing, they gets better grub than [...] you let me catch you chuckin' stuff over the f[...] 'av you arrested for fraternisin' with the ene[...] before I changes me mind.'

The guardroom had turned out, an officer[...] with the leader through the wire. The e[...] made our trudge to the boring City of Ox[...]

The Vicar never tired of telling us o[...] university. As one patrol leader comm[...] come from you could get six months fo[...] he did.'

Oxford held no charms for us boys. W[...] do scouting things around camp. The[...]

got tighter, bread went on the ration, my Dad complained about the amount of bran in the standard loaf.

My Mother quick as light said, 'Horses seem to thrive on it.'

My last holiday with the Scouts at Camp Sea Ash, Suffolk was memorable for two things.

1) The dropping of the atomic bombs on Japan. Reading the newspapers we gathered that there was nowhere to hide, the Top Brass were just as likely to 'fry' as the lower orders. 2) We spent many happy hours beach combing. Dire warnings were issued about landmines that had been sown during the invasion scare in 40 and 41. They had to be lifted by hand. That delicate task fell to POWs. The detritus of war including drop tanks littered the beaches. The drop tanks held approximately forty gallons, giving an aircraft increased range.

When the plane approached the Belgian coast, the tank was dropped, time and tide drifted them over to our beaches, where enterprising members of the Home Guard siphoned the mix of sea water and petrol out of the tank, to be filtered and sold on the Black Market.

I think the lorry and the Morris Eight ran home on the stuff, the lorry driver had to strip down both carbs on the car and the lorry several times – the high spot of the holiday for us boys. I overheard the Vicar say to the lorry driver, 'This wretched war is making criminals of us all.'

The lorry driver laughed. 'If you don't say nothing Vicar, I won't.'

Motor repairs sure beat looking at Wool Churches, after all there are at least half a dozen a short bike ride from Northolt better than these. The Vicar was in ecstasies over the churches, he seemed oblivious to the fooling about going on, but then he had his back to us.

When I got home I thought I would impress my parents with my knowledge of the Wool Churches.

My Dad cut my lecture short. 'Before they had the sheep the Church lived off the backs of the peasants, when they had the

sheep they lived off the backs of the peasants and the sheep.'
Where upon my Dad folded his newspaper and put it in the
rack.

Never mind, next time I go up to Uncle George's house, I
will get him chatting about the scout camp and he will give
me the 'Pukka GEN'.

Work

I had been thinking about the future for some time, everyone
gave me the same advice. Get a trade. I was doing quite well,
gardening and working for Mr Stevens at weekends, toasters
and irons held no mysteries for me. Simple faults on wireless
were within my grasp, thanks to a book John's Dad bought
me for my birthday. My Dad paid an annual subscription for
Practical Wireless, a monthly magazine.

Of course, I didn't tell Mr Stevens about the book and the
magazine, he was very cagey and gave away very little information. I suppose he saw me as a future competitor, he did
subscribe to *Wireless World* which talked about television and
stuff well above my head, and his.

Mrs Stevens used to bring cakes and tea out to the workshop, she would sit and talk. I gathered that theirs was a
loveless marriage. She often remarked that he loved the dog
but tolerated her. She seemed to be a very lonely lady.

I listened and made the right noises such as, 'Oh how awful,
you don't say!' and so on. I became quite adept at being able
to sort of listen and work.

One tea break she said casually, 'Have you thought about
what you will do when you leave school?'

'Not really,' I lied. I thought of little else.

'Well you should, I don't know if you have noticed Jim has taken on more work, if you want a job when you leave school there is one waiting here for you.'

'There is a problem, I am fourteen in January therefore I cannot leave school until August.'

'We have thought of that, when the truant man calls on your parents as he most certainly will, you will refuse to tell him where you are working also, try as they might your parents have been unable to persuade you to go to school.'

'What do you do all day?'

'Your reply: Casual work.'

'Where?'

'All over the place. There is no shortage.'

And so on and so on, every tea break it was the same, until she said, 'Would you ask your Mum if she would like to pop round for a cup of tea next Sunday afternoon, on her own?'

To cut a long story short, the truant officer did call at our house, interviewed me several times on my own and with my Mother present. I was never rude to him or guilty of dumb insolence, eventually he announced that this would be his last visit.

My Father was summoned from the back room. We all shook hands, then he paused. 'I wonder if I might book another appointment in say ten years' time.' He inclined his head and smiled. My Father laughed.

'We are as curious about his future as you are, Sir. However, we do feel that he will come good.'

I did not come good, I came 'not bad,' all things considered. I had two prerequisites on my side, strong clever women and bags of luck!

L - #0122 - 110920 - C0 - 210/148/5 - PB - DID2905719